CAREER EXAMINATION SERIES

THIS IS YOUR **PASSBOOK**® FOR ...

MANAGER, INFORMATION TECHNOLOGY SERVICES I

NATIONAL LEARNING CORPORATION®
passbooks.com

PASSBOOK® SERIES

THE *PASSBOOK® SERIES* has been created to prepare applicants and candidates for the ultimate academic battlefield – the examination room.

At some time in our lives, each and every one of us may be required to take an examination – for validation, matriculation, admission, qualification, registration, certification, or licensure.

Based on the assumption that every applicant or candidate has met the basic formal educational standards, has taken the required number of courses, and read the necessary texts, the *PASSBOOK® SERIES* furnishes the one special preparation which may assure passing with confidence, instead of failing with insecurity. Examination questions – together with answers – are furnished as the basic vehicle for study so that the mysteries of the examination and its compounding difficulties may be eliminated or diminished by a sure method.

This book is meant to help you pass your examination provided that you qualify and are serious in your objective.

The entire field is reviewed through the huge store of content information which is succinctly presented through a provocative and challenging approach – the question-and-answer method.

A climate of success is established by furnishing the correct answers at the end of each test.

You soon learn to recognize types of questions, forms of questions, and patterns of questioning. You may even begin to anticipate expected outcomes.

You perceive that many questions are repeated or adapted so that you can gain acute insights, which may enable you to score many sure points.

You learn how to confront new questions, or types of questions, and to attack them confidently and work out the correct answers.

You note objectives and emphases, and recognize pitfalls and dangers, so that you may make positive educational adjustments.

Moreover, you are kept fully informed in relation to new concepts, methods, practices, and directions in the field.

You discover that you arre actually taking the examination all the time: you are preparing for the examination by "taking" an examination, not by reading extraneous and/or supererogatory textbooks.

In short, this PASSBOOK®, used directedly, should be an important factor in helping you to pass your test.

MANAGER, INFORMATION TECHNOLOGY SERVICES I

DUTIES

As a Manager Information Technology Services I, you would plan, direct and coordinate systems analysis, design, and application program development, maintenance, implementation and quality assurance activities.

As a Manager Information Technology Services I (Database), you would plan, direct and coordinate database design, development, installation and maintenance activities.

As a Manager Information Technology Services I (Data Communications), you would plan, direct and coordinate data communications activities including network design, analysis, capacity planning, installation, monitoring and maintenance.

As a Manager Information Technology Services I (Operations), you would plan, direct, and coordinate computer operations activities including all data processing hardware and peripheral equipment operation.

As a Manager Information Technology Services I (Systems Programming), you would plan, direct and coordinate systems programming activities including the design, development, acquisition, modification, installation and maintenance of system software.

As a Manager Information Technology Services I (Technical), you would plan, direct and coordinate activities in any combination of two or more of the Information Resource Management (IRM) technical specialties. The specialties include database, data communications, operations and systems programming.

SCOPE OF THE EXAMINATION

The written test is designed to test for knowledge, skills, and/or abilities in such areas as:

1. **Administration** - These questions test for knowledge of the managerial functions involved in directing an organization or an organizational segment. These questions cover such areas as: developing objectives and formulating policies; making decisions based on the context of the administrator's position and authority; forecasting and planning, including succession planning; organizing; developing personnel; coordinating and informing; guiding and leading; testing and evaluating; and budgeting.
2. **Project management fundamentals** - These questions test for knowledge of the techniques and concepts of project management. They may cover terminology and concepts; project scheduling and control techniques (e.g., CPM); creating and evaluating bids; monitoring project progress; controlling a project timeline; and evaluating the project.
3. **Supervision** - These questions test for knowledge of the principles and practices employed in planning, organizing, and controlling the activities of a work unit toward predetermined objectives. The concepts covered, usually in a situational question format, include such topics as assigning and reviewing work; evaluating performance; maintaining work standards; motivating and developing subordinates; implementing procedural change; increasing efficiency; and dealing with problems of absenteeism, morale, and discipline.

4. **Systems Analysis** - These questions test for techniques and concepts of computer systems analysis. They cover such subjects as feasibility and applications studies, systems development tools and software, the systems life cycle, types of systems (e.g., client/server, Web-based), controls, and systems documentation, testing, and implementation.

5. **Understanding and interpreting tabular material** - These questions test your ability to understand, analyze, and use the internal logic of data presented in tabular form. You may be asked to perform tasks such as completing tables, drawing conclusions from them, analyzing data trends or interrelationships, and revising or combining data sets. The concepts of rate, ratio, and proportion are tested. Mathematical operations are simple, and computational speed is not a major factor in the test.

6. **Writing skills for managers** - These questions test for the writing skills that managers use in composing their own reports and correspondence as well as in reviewing documents produced by others. Both sentence skills and paragraph skills are addressed. The specific points tested include grammar, usage, punctuation, and sentence structure, appropriate and correct content, editing, and organizing sentences into well-constructed paragraphs.

HOW TO TAKE A TEST

I. YOU MUST PASS AN EXAMINATION

A. *WHAT EVERY CANDIDATE SHOULD KNOW*

Examination applicants often ask us for help in preparing for the written test. What can I study in advance? What kinds of questions will be asked? How will the test be given? How will the papers be graded?

As an applicant for a civil service examination, you may be wondering about some of these things. Our purpose here is to suggest effective methods of advance study and to describe civil service examinations.

Your chances for success on this examination can be increased if you know how to prepare. Those "pre-examination jitters" can be reduced if you know what to expect. You can even experience an adventure in good citizenship if you know why civil service exams are given.

B. *WHY ARE CIVIL SERVICE EXAMINATIONS GIVEN?*

Civil service examinations are important to you in two ways. As a citizen, you want public jobs filled by employees who know how to do their work. As a job seeker, you want a fair chance to compete for that job on an equal footing with other candidates. The best-known means of accomplishing this two-fold goal is the competitive examination.

Exams are widely publicized throughout the nation. They may be administered for jobs in federal, state, city, municipal, town or village governments or agencies.

Any citizen may apply, with some limitations, such as the age or residence of applicants. Your experience and education may be reviewed to see whether you meet the requirements for the particular examination. When these requirements exist, they are reasonable and applied consistently to all applicants. Thus, a competitive examination may cause you some uneasiness now, but it is your privilege and safeguard.

C. *HOW ARE CIVIL SERVICE EXAMS DEVELOPED?*

Examinations are carefully written by trained technicians who are specialists in the field known as "psychological measurement," in consultation with recognized authorities in the field of work that the test will cover. These experts recommend the subject matter areas or skills to be tested; only those knowledges or skills important to your success on the job are included. The most reliable books and source materials available are used as references. Together, the experts and technicians judge the difficulty level of the questions.

Test technicians know how to phrase questions so that the problem is clearly stated. Their ethics do not permit "trick" or "catch" questions. Questions may have been tried out on sample groups, or subjected to statistical analysis, to determine their usefulness.

Written tests are often used in combination with performance tests, ratings of training and experience, and oral interviews. All of these measures combine to form the best-known means of finding the right person for the right job.

II. HOW TO PASS THE WRITTEN TEST

A. NATURE OF THE EXAMINATION

To prepare intelligently for civil service examinations, you should know how they differ from school examinations you have taken. In school you were assigned certain definite pages to read or subjects to cover. The examination questions were quite detailed and usually emphasized memory. Civil service exams, on the other hand, try to discover your present ability to perform the duties of a position, plus your potentiality to learn these duties. In other words, a civil service exam attempts to predict how successful you will be. Questions cover such a broad area that they cannot be as minute and detailed as school exam questions.

In the public service similar kinds of work, or positions, are grouped together in one "class." This process is known as *position-classification*. All the positions in a class are paid according to the salary range for that class. One class title covers all of these positions, and they are all tested by the same examination.

B. FOUR BASIC STEPS

1) Study the announcement

How, then, can you know what subjects to study? Our best answer is: "Learn as much as possible about the class of positions for which you've applied." The exam will test the knowledge, skills and abilities needed to do the work.

Your most valuable source of information about the position you want is the official exam announcement. This announcement lists the training and experience qualifications. Check these standards and apply only if you come reasonably close to meeting them.

The brief description of the position in the examination announcement offers some clues to the subjects which will be tested. Think about the job itself. Review the duties in your mind. Can you perform them, or are there some in which you are rusty? Fill in the blank spots in your preparation.

Many jurisdictions preview the written test in the exam announcement by including a section called "Knowledge and Abilities Required," "Scope of the Examination," or some similar heading. Here you will find out specifically what fields will be tested.

2) Review your own background

Once you learn in general what the position is all about, and what you need to know to do the work, ask yourself which subjects you already know fairly well and which need improvement. You may wonder whether to concentrate on improving your strong areas or on building some background in your fields of weakness. When the announcement has specified "some knowledge" or "considerable knowledge," or has used adjectives like "beginning principles of…" or "advanced … methods," you can get a clue as to the number and difficulty of questions to be asked in any given field. More questions, and hence broader coverage, would be included for those subjects which are more important in the work. Now weigh your strengths and weaknesses against the job requirements and prepare accordingly.

3) Determine the level of the position

Another way to tell how intensively you should prepare is to understand the level of the job for which you are applying. Is it the entering level? In other words, is this the position in which beginners in a field of work are hired? Or is it an intermediate or advanced level? Sometimes this is indicated by such words as "Junior" or "Senior" in the class title. Other jurisdictions use Roman numerals to designate the level – Clerk I, Clerk II, for example. The word "Supervisor" sometimes appears in the title. If the level is not indicated by the title, check the description of duties. Will you be working under very close supervision, or will you have responsibility for independent decisions in this work?

4) Choose appropriate study materials

Now that you know the subjects to be examined and the relative amount of each subject to be covered, you can choose suitable study materials. For beginning level jobs, or even advanced ones, if you have a pronounced weakness in some aspect of your training, read a modern, standard textbook in that field. Be sure it is up to date and has general coverage. Such books are normally available at your library, and the librarian will be glad to help you locate one. For entry-level positions, questions of appropriate difficulty are chosen – neither highly advanced questions, nor those too simple. Such questions require careful thought but not advanced training.

If the position for which you are applying is technical or advanced, you will read more advanced, specialized material. If you are already familiar with the basic principles of your field, elementary textbooks would waste your time. Concentrate on advanced textbooks and technical periodicals. Think through the concepts and review difficult problems in your field.

These are all general sources. You can get more ideas on your own initiative, following these leads. For example, training manuals and publications of the government agency which employs workers in your field can be useful, particularly for technical and professional positions. A letter or visit to the government department involved may result in more specific study suggestions, and certainly will provide you with a more definite idea of the exact nature of the position you are seeking.

III. KINDS OF TESTS

Tests are used for purposes other than measuring knowledge and ability to perform specified duties. For some positions, it is equally important to test ability to make adjustments to new situations or to profit from training. In others, basic mental abilities not dependent on information are essential. Questions which test these things may not appear as pertinent to the duties of the position as those which test for knowledge and information. Yet they are often highly important parts of a fair examination. For very general questions, it is almost impossible to help you direct your study efforts. What we can do is to point out some of the more common of these general abilities needed in public service positions and describe some typical questions.

1) General information

Broad, general information has been found useful for predicting job success in some kinds of work. This is tested in a variety of ways, from vocabulary lists to questions about current events. Basic background in some field of work, such as sociology or economics, may be sampled in a group of questions. Often these are principles which have become familiar to most persons through exposure rather than through formal training. It is difficult to advise you how to study for these questions; being alert to the world around you is our best suggestion.

2) Verbal ability

An example of an ability needed in many positions is verbal or language ability. Verbal ability is, in brief, the ability to use and understand words. Vocabulary and grammar tests are typical measures of this ability. Reading comprehension or paragraph interpretation questions are common in many kinds of civil service tests. You are given a paragraph of written material and asked to find its central meaning.

3) Numerical ability

Number skills can be tested by the familiar arithmetic problem, by checking paired lists of numbers to see which are alike and which are different, or by interpreting charts and graphs. In the latter test, a graph may be printed in the test booklet which you are asked to use as the basis for answering questions.

4) Observation

A popular test for law-enforcement positions is the observation test. A picture is shown to you for several minutes, then taken away. Questions about the picture test your ability to observe both details and larger elements.

5) Following directions

In many positions in the public service, the employee must be able to carry out written instructions dependably and accurately. You may be given a chart with several columns, each column listing a variety of information. The questions require you to carry out directions involving the information given in the chart.

6) Skills and aptitudes

Performance tests effectively measure some manual skills and aptitudes. When the skill is one in which you are trained, such as typing or shorthand, you can practice. These tests are often very much like those given in business school or high school courses. For many of the other skills and aptitudes, however, no short-time preparation can be made. Skills and abilities natural to you or that you have developed throughout your lifetime are being tested.

Many of the general questions just described provide all the data needed to answer the questions and ask you to use your reasoning ability to find the answers. Your best preparation for these tests, as well as for tests of facts and ideas, is to be at your physical and mental best. You, no doubt, have your own methods of getting into an exam-taking mood and keeping "in shape." The next section lists some ideas on this subject.

IV. KINDS OF QUESTIONS

Only rarely is the "essay" question, which you answer in narrative form, used in civil service tests. Civil service tests are usually of the short-answer type. Full instructions for answering these questions will be given to you at the examination. But in case this is your first experience with short-answer questions and separate answer sheets, here is what you need to know:

1) Multiple-choice Questions

Most popular of the short-answer questions is the "multiple choice" or "best answer" question. It can be used, for example, to test for factual knowledge, ability to solve problems or judgment in meeting situations found at work.

A multiple-choice question is normally one of three types—

- It can begin with an incomplete statement followed by several possible endings. You are to find the one ending which *best* completes the statement, although some of the others may not be entirely wrong.
- It can also be a complete statement in the form of a question which is answered by choosing one of the statements listed.
- It can be in the form of a problem – again you select the best answer.

Here is an example of a multiple-choice question with a discussion which should give you some clues as to the method for choosing the right answer:

When an employee has a complaint about his assignment, the action which will *best* help him overcome his difficulty is to
  A. discuss his difficulty with his coworkers
  B. take the problem to the head of the organization
  C. take the problem to the person who gave him the assignment
  D. say nothing to anyone about his complaint

In answering this question, you should study each of the choices to find which is best. Consider choice "A" – Certainly an employee may discuss his complaint with fellow employees, but no change or improvement can result, and the complaint remains unresolved. Choice "B" is a poor choice since the head of the organization probably does not know what assignment you have been given, and taking your problem to him is known as "going over the head" of the supervisor. The supervisor, or person who made the assignment, is the person who can clarify it or correct any injustice. Choice "C" is, therefore, correct. To say nothing, as in choice "D," is unwise. Supervisors have and interest in knowing the problems employees are facing, and the employee is seeking a solution to his problem.

2) True/False Questions

The "true/false" or "right/wrong" form of question is sometimes used. Here a complete statement is given. Your job is to decide whether the statement is right or wrong.

SAMPLE: A roaming cell-phone call to a nearby city costs less than a non-roaming call to a distant city.

This statement is wrong, or false, since roaming calls are more expensive.

This is not a complete list of all possible question forms, although most of the others are variations of these common types. You will always get complete directions for answering questions. Be sure you understand *how* to mark your answers – ask questions until you do.

V. RECORDING YOUR ANSWERS

Computer terminals are used more and more today for many different kinds of exams.

For an examination with very few applicants, you may be told to record your answers in the test booklet itself. Separate answer sheets are much more common. If this separate answer sheet is to be scored by machine – and this is often the case – it is highly important that you mark your answers correctly in order to get credit.

An electronic scoring machine is often used in civil service offices because of the speed with which papers can be scored. Machine-scored answer sheets must be marked with a pencil, which will be given to you. This pencil has a high graphite content which responds to the electronic scoring machine. As a matter of fact, stray dots may register as answers, so do not let your pencil rest on the answer sheet while you are pondering the correct answer. Also, if your pencil lead breaks or is otherwise defective, ask for another.

Since the answer sheet will be dropped in a slot in the scoring machine, be careful not to bend the corners or get the paper crumpled.

The answer sheet normally has five vertical columns of numbers, with 30 numbers to a column. These numbers correspond to the question numbers in your test booklet. After each number, going across the page are four or five pairs of dotted lines. These short dotted lines have small letters or numbers above them. The first two pairs may also have a "T" or "F" above the letters. This indicates that the first two pairs only are to be used if the questions are of the true-false type. If the questions are multiple choice, disregard the "T" and "F" and pay attention only to the small letters or numbers.

Answer your questions in the manner of the sample that follows:

32. The largest city in the United States is
    A. Washington, D.C.
    B. New York City
    C. Chicago
    D. Detroit
    E. San Francisco

1) Choose the answer you think is best. (New York City is the largest, so "B" is correct.)
2) Find the row of dotted lines numbered the same as the question you are answering. (Find row number 32)
3) Find the pair of dotted lines corresponding to the answer. (Find the pair of lines under the mark "B.")
4) Make a solid black mark between the dotted lines.

VI. BEFORE THE TEST

Common sense will help you find procedures to follow to get ready for an examination. Too many of us, however, overlook these sensible measures. Indeed, nervousness and fatigue have been found to be the most serious reasons why applicants fail to do their best on civil service tests. Here is a list of reminders:

- Begin your preparation early – Don't wait until the last minute to go scurrying around for books and materials or to find out what the position is all about.
- Prepare continuously – An hour a night for a week is better than an all-night cram session. This has been definitely established. What is more, a night a week for a month will return better dividends than crowding your study into a shorter period of time.
- Locate the place of the exam – You have been sent a notice telling you when and where to report for the examination. If the location is in a different town or otherwise unfamiliar to you, it would be well to inquire the best route and learn something about the building.
- Relax the night before the test – Allow your mind to rest. Do not study at all that night. Plan some mild recreation or diversion; then go to bed early and get a good night's sleep.
- Get up early enough to make a leisurely trip to the place for the test – This way unforeseen events, traffic snarls, unfamiliar buildings, etc. will not upset you.
- Dress comfortably – A written test is not a fashion show. You will be known by number and not by name, so wear something comfortable.
- Leave excess paraphernalia at home – Shopping bags and odd bundles will get in your way. You need bring only the items mentioned in the official notice you received; usually everything you need is provided. Do not bring reference books to the exam. They will only confuse those last minutes and be taken away from you when in the test room.
- Arrive somewhat ahead of time – If because of transportation schedules you must get there very early, bring a newspaper or magazine to take your mind off yourself while waiting.
- Locate the examination room – When you have found the proper room, you will be directed to the seat or part of the room where you will sit. Sometimes you are given a sheet of instructions to read while you are waiting. Do not fill out any forms until you are told to do so; just read them and be prepared.
- Relax and prepare to listen to the instructions
- If you have any physical problem that may keep you from doing your best, be sure to tell the test administrator. If you are sick or in poor health, you really cannot do your best on the exam. You can come back and take the test some other time.

VII. AT THE TEST

The day of the test is here and you have the test booklet in your hand. The temptation to get going is very strong. Caution! There is more to success than knowing the right answers. You must know how to identify your papers and understand variations in the type of short-answer question used in this particular examination. Follow these suggestions for maximum results from your efforts:

1) Cooperate with the monitor

The test administrator has a duty to create a situation in which you can be as much at ease as possible. He will give instructions, tell you when to begin, check to see that you are marking your answer sheet correctly, and so on. He is not there to guard you, although he will see that your competitors do not take unfair advantage. He wants to help you do your best.

2) Listen to all instructions

Don't jump the gun! Wait until you understand all directions. In most civil service tests you get more time than you need to answer the questions. So don't be in a hurry. Read each word of instructions until you clearly understand the meaning. Study the examples, listen to all announcements and follow directions. Ask questions if you do not understand what to do.

3) Identify your papers

Civil service exams are usually identified by number only. You will be assigned a number; you must not put your name on your test papers. Be sure to copy your number correctly. Since more than one exam may be given, copy your exact examination title.

4) Plan your time

Unless you are told that a test is a "speed" or "rate of work" test, speed itself is usually not important. Time enough to answer all the questions will be provided, but this does not mean that you have all day. An overall time limit has been set. Divide the total time (in minutes) by the number of questions to determine the approximate time you have for each question.

5) Do not linger over difficult questions

If you come across a difficult question, mark it with a paper clip (useful to have along) and come back to it when you have been through the booklet. One caution if you do this – be sure to skip a number on your answer sheet as well. Check often to be sure that you have not lost your place and that you are marking in the row numbered the same as the question you are answering.

6) Read the questions

Be sure you know what the question asks! Many capable people are unsuccessful because they failed to *read* the questions correctly.

7) Answer all questions

Unless you have been instructed that a penalty will be deducted for incorrect answers, it is better to guess than to omit a question.

8) Speed tests

It is often better NOT to guess on speed tests. It has been found that on timed tests people are tempted to spend the last few seconds before time is called in marking answers at random – without even reading them – in the hope of picking up a few extra points. To discourage this practice, the instructions may warn you that your score will be "corrected" for guessing. That is, a penalty will be applied. The incorrect answers will be deducted from the correct ones, or some other penalty formula will be used.

9) Review your answers

If you finish before time is called, go back to the questions you guessed or omitted to give them further thought. Review other answers if you have time.

10) Return your test materials

If you are ready to leave before others have finished or time is called, take ALL your materials to the monitor and leave quietly. Never take any test material with you. The monitor can discover whose papers are not complete, and taking a test booklet may be grounds for disqualification.

VIII. EXAMINATION TECHNIQUES

1) Read the general instructions carefully. These are usually printed on the first page of the exam booklet. As a rule, these instructions refer to the timing of the examination; the fact that you should not start work until the signal and must stop work at a signal, etc. If there are any *special* instructions, such as a choice of questions to be answered, make sure that you note this instruction carefully.

2) When you are ready to start work on the examination, that is as soon as the signal has been given, read the instructions to each question booklet, underline any key words or phrases, such as *least, best, outline, describe* and the like. In this way you will tend to answer as requested rather than discover on reviewing your paper that you *listed without describing*, that you selected the *worst* choice rather than the *best* choice, etc.

3) If the examination is of the objective or multiple-choice type – that is, each question will also give a series of possible answers: A, B, C or D, and you are called upon to select the best answer and write the letter next to that answer on your answer paper – it is advisable to start answering each question in turn. There may be anywhere from 50 to 100 such questions in the three or four hours allotted and you can see how much time would be taken if you read through all the questions before beginning to answer any. Furthermore, if you come across a question or group of questions which you know would be difficult to answer, it would undoubtedly affect your handling of all the other questions.

4) If the examination is of the essay type and contains but a few questions, it is a moot point as to whether you should read all the questions before starting to answer any one. Of course, if you are given a choice – say five out of seven and the like – then it is essential to read all the questions so you can eliminate the two that are most difficult. If, however, you are asked to answer all the questions, there may be danger in trying to answer the easiest one first because you may find that you will spend too much time on it. The best technique is to answer the first question, then proceed to the second, etc.

5) Time your answers. Before the exam begins, write down the time it started, then add the time allowed for the examination and write down the time it must be completed, then divide the time available somewhat as follows:

- If 3-1/2 hours are allowed, that would be 210 minutes. If you have 80 objective-type questions, that would be an average of 2-1/2 minutes per question. Allow yourself no more than 2 minutes per question, or a total of 160 minutes, which will permit about 50 minutes to review.
- If for the time allotment of 210 minutes there are 7 essay questions to answer, that would average about 30 minutes a question. Give yourself only 25 minutes per question so that you have about 35 minutes to review.

6) The most important instruction is to *read each question* and make sure you know what is wanted. The second most important instruction is to *time yourself properly* so that you answer every question. The third most important instruction is to *answer every question*. Guess if you have to but include something for each question. Remember that you will receive no credit for a blank and will probably receive some credit if you write something in answer to an essay question. If you guess a letter – say "B" for a multiple-choice question – you may have guessed right. If you leave a blank as an answer to a multiple-choice question, the examiners may respect your feelings but it will not add a point to your score. Some exams may penalize you for wrong answers, so in such cases *only*, you may not want to guess unless you have some basis for your answer.

7) Suggestions
   a. Objective-type questions
      1. Examine the question booklet for proper sequence of pages and questions
      2. Read all instructions carefully
      3. Skip any question which seems too difficult; return to it after all other questions have been answered
      4. Apportion your time properly; do not spend too much time on any single question or group of questions
      5. Note and underline key words – *all, most, fewest, least, best, worst, same, opposite,* etc.
      6. Pay particular attention to negatives
      7. Note unusual option, e.g., unduly long, short, complex, different or similar in content to the body of the question
      8. Observe the use of "hedging" words – *probably, may, most likely,* etc.
      9. Make sure that your answer is put next to the same number as the question
      10. Do not second-guess unless you have good reason to believe the second answer is definitely more correct
      11. Cross out original answer if you decide another answer is more accurate; do not erase until you are ready to hand your paper in
      12. Answer all questions; guess unless instructed otherwise
      13. Leave time for review

   b. Essay questions
      1. Read each question carefully
      2. Determine exactly what is wanted. Underline key words or phrases.
      3. Decide on outline or paragraph answer

4. Include many different points and elements unless asked to develop any one or two points or elements
5. Show impartiality by giving pros and cons unless directed to select one side only
6. Make and write down any assumptions you find necessary to answer the questions
7. Watch your English, grammar, punctuation and choice of words
8. Time your answers; don't crowd material

8) Answering the essay question

Most essay questions can be answered by framing the specific response around several key words or ideas. Here are a few such key words or ideas:

M's: manpower, materials, methods, money, management
P's: purpose, program, policy, plan, procedure, practice, problems, pitfalls, personnel, public relations
   a. Six basic steps in handling problems:
      1. Preliminary plan and background development
      2. Collect information, data and facts
      3. Analyze and interpret information, data and facts
      4. Analyze and develop solutions as well as make recommendations
      5. Prepare report and sell recommendations
      6. Install recommendations and follow up effectiveness

   b. Pitfalls to avoid
      1. *Taking things for granted* – A statement of the situation does not necessarily imply that each of the elements is necessarily true; for example, a complaint may be invalid and biased so that all that can be taken for granted is that a complaint has been registered
      2. *Considering only one side of a situation* – Wherever possible, indicate several alternatives and then point out the reasons you selected the best one
      3. *Failing to indicate follow up* – Whenever your answer indicates action on your part, make certain that you will take proper follow-up action to see how successful your recommendations, procedures or actions turn out to be
      4. *Taking too long in answering any single question* – Remember to time your answers properly

IX. AFTER THE TEST

Scoring procedures differ in detail among civil service jurisdictions although the general principles are the same. Whether the papers are hand-scored or graded by machine we have described, they are nearly always graded by number. That is, the person who marks the paper knows only the number – never the name – of the applicant. Not until all the papers have been graded will they be matched with names. If other tests, such as training and experience or oral interview ratings have been given, scores will be combined. Different parts of the examination usually have different weights. For example, the written test might count 60 percent of the final grade, and a rating of training and experience 40 percent. In many jurisdictions, veterans will have a certain number of points added to their grades.

After the final grade has been determined, the names are placed in grade order and an eligible list is established. There are various methods for resolving ties between those who get the same final grade – probably the most common is to place first the name of the person whose application was received first. Job offers are made from the eligible list in the order the names appear on it. You will be notified of your grade and your rank as soon as all these computations have been made. This will be done as rapidly as possible.

People who are found to meet the requirements in the announcement are called "eligibles." Their names are put on a list of eligible candidates. An eligible's chances of getting a job depend on how high he stands on this list and how fast agencies are filling jobs from the list.

When a job is to be filled from a list of eligibles, the agency asks for the names of people on the list of eligibles for that job. When the civil service commission receives this request, it sends to the agency the names of the three people highest on this list. Or, if the job to be filled has specialized requirements, the office sends the agency the names of the top three persons who meet these requirements from the general list.

The appointing officer makes a choice from among the three people whose names were sent to him. If the selected person accepts the appointment, the names of the others are put back on the list to be considered for future openings.

That is the rule in hiring from all kinds of eligible lists, whether they are for typist, carpenter, chemist, or something else. For every vacancy, the appointing officer has his choice of any one of the top three eligibles on the list. This explains why the person whose name is on top of the list sometimes does not get an appointment when some of the persons lower on the list do. If the appointing officer chooses the second or third eligible, the No. 1 eligible does not get a job at once, but stays on the list until he is appointed or the list is terminated.

X. HOW TO PASS THE INTERVIEW TEST

The examination for which you applied requires an oral interview test. You have already taken the written test and you are now being called for the interview test – the final part of the formal examination.

You may think that it is not possible to prepare for an interview test and that there are no procedures to follow during an interview. Our purpose is to point out some things you can do in advance that will help you and some good rules to follow and pitfalls to avoid while you are being interviewed.

What is an interview supposed to test?

The written examination is designed to test the technical knowledge and competence of the candidate; the oral is designed to evaluate intangible qualities, not readily measured otherwise, and to establish a list showing the relative fitness of each candidate – as measured against his competitors – for the position sought. Scoring is not on the basis of "right" and "wrong," but on a sliding scale of values ranging from "not passable" to "outstanding." As a matter of fact, it is possible to achieve a relatively low score without a single "incorrect" answer because of evident weakness in the qualities being measured.

Occasionally, an examination may consist entirely of an oral test – either an individual or a group oral. In such cases, information is sought concerning the technical knowledges and abilities of the candidate, since there has been no written examination for this purpose. More commonly, however, an oral test is used to supplement a written examination.

Who conducts interviews?

The composition of oral boards varies among different jurisdictions. In nearly all, a representative of the personnel department serves as chairman. One of the members of the board may be a representative of the department in which the candidate would work. In some cases, "outside experts" are used, and, frequently, a businessman or some other representative of the general public is asked to serve. Labor and management or other special groups may be represented. The aim is to secure the services of experts in the appropriate field.

However the board is composed, it is a good idea (and not at all improper or unethical) to ascertain in advance of the interview who the members are and what groups they represent. When you are introduced to them, you will have some idea of their backgrounds and interests, and at least you will not stutter and stammer over their names.

What should be done before the interview?

While knowledge about the board members is useful and takes some of the surprise element out of the interview, there is other preparation which is more substantive. It *is* possible to prepare for an oral interview – in several ways:

1) Keep a copy of your application and review it carefully before the interview

This may be the only document before the oral board, and the starting point of the interview. Know what education and experience you have listed there, and the sequence and dates of all of it. Sometimes the board will ask you to review the highlights of your experience for them; you should not have to hem and haw doing it.

2) Study the class specification and the examination announcement

Usually, the oral board has one or both of these to guide them. The qualities, characteristics or knowledges required by the position sought are stated in these documents. They offer valuable clues as to the nature of the oral interview. For example, if the job involves supervisory responsibilities, the announcement will usually indicate that knowledge of modern supervisory methods and the qualifications of the candidate as a supervisor will be tested. If so, you can expect such questions, frequently in the form of a hypothetical situation which you are expected to solve. NEVER go into an oral without knowledge of the duties and responsibilities of the job you seek.

3) Think through each qualification required

Try to visualize the kind of questions you would ask if you were a board member. How well could you answer them? Try especially to appraise your own knowledge and background in each area, *measured against the job sought*, and identify any areas in which you are weak. Be critical and realistic – do not flatter yourself.

4) Do some general reading in areas in which you feel you may be weak

For example, if the job involves supervision and your past experience has NOT, some general reading in supervisory methods and practices, particularly in the field of human relations, might be useful. Do NOT study agency procedures or detailed manuals. The oral board will be testing your understanding and capacity, not your memory.

5) Get a good night's sleep and watch your general health and mental attitude

You will want a clear head at the interview. Take care of a cold or any other minor ailment, and of course, no hangovers.

What should be done on the day of the interview?

Now comes the day of the interview itself. Give yourself plenty of time to get there. Plan to arrive somewhat ahead of the scheduled time, particularly if your appointment is in the fore part of the day. If a previous candidate fails to appear, the board might be ready for you a bit early. By early afternoon an oral board is almost invariably behind schedule if there are many candidates, and you may have to wait. Take along a book or magazine to read, or your application to review, but leave any extraneous material in the waiting room when you go in for your interview. In any event, relax and compose yourself.

The matter of dress is important. The board is forming impressions about you – from your experience, your manners, your attitude, and your appearance. Give your personal appearance careful attention. Dress your best, but not your flashiest. Choose conservative, appropriate clothing, and be sure it is immaculate. This is a business interview, and your appearance should indicate that you regard it as such. Besides, being well groomed and properly dressed will help boost your confidence.

Sooner or later, someone will call your name and escort you into the interview room. *This is it.* From here on you are on your own. It is too late for any more preparation. But remember, you asked for this opportunity to prove your fitness, and you are here because your request was granted.

What happens when you go in?

The usual sequence of events will be as follows: The clerk (who is often the board stenographer) will introduce you to the chairman of the oral board, who will introduce you to the other members of the board. Acknowledge the introductions before you sit down. Do not be surprised if you find a microphone facing you or a stenotypist sitting by. Oral interviews are usually recorded in the event of an appeal or other review.

Usually the chairman of the board will open the interview by reviewing the highlights of your education and work experience from your application – primarily for the benefit of the other members of the board, as well as to get the material into the record. Do not interrupt or comment unless there is an error or significant misinterpretation; if that is the case, do not hesitate. But do not quibble about insignificant matters. Also, he will usually ask you some question about your education, experience or your present job – partly to get you to start talking and to establish the interviewing "rapport." He may start the actual questioning, or turn it over to one of the other members. Frequently, each member undertakes the questioning on a particular area, one in which he is perhaps most competent, so you can expect each member to participate in the examination. Because time is limited, you may also expect some rather abrupt switches in the direction the questioning takes, so do not be upset by it. Normally, a board member will not pursue a single line of questioning unless he discovers a particular strength or weakness.

After each member has participated, the chairman will usually ask whether any member has any further questions, then will ask you if you have anything you wish to add. Unless you are expecting this question, it may floor you. Worse, it may start you off on an extended, extemporaneous speech. The board is not usually seeking more information. The question is principally to offer you a last opportunity to present further qualifications or to indicate that you have nothing to add. So, if you feel that a significant qualification or characteristic has been overlooked, it is proper to point it out in a sentence or so. Do not compliment the board on the thoroughness of their examination – they have been sketchy, and you know it. If you wish, merely say, "No thank you, I have nothing further to add." This is a point where you can "talk yourself out" of a good impression or fail to present an important bit of information. Remember, *you close the interview yourself.*

The chairman will then say, "That is all, Mr. _____, thank you." Do not be startled; the interview is over, and quicker than you think. Thank him, gather your belongings and take your leave. Save your sigh of relief for the other side of the door.

How to put your best foot forward

Throughout this entire process, you may feel that the board individually and collectively is trying to pierce your defenses, seek out your hidden weaknesses and embarrass and confuse you. Actually, this is not true. They are obliged to make an appraisal of your qualifications for the job you are seeking, and they want to see you in your best light. Remember, they must interview all candidates and a non-cooperative candidate may become a failure in spite of their best efforts to bring out his qualifications. Here are 15 suggestions that will help you:

1) Be natural – Keep your attitude confident, not cocky

If you are not confident that you can do the job, do not expect the board to be. Do not apologize for your weaknesses, try to bring out your strong points. The board is interested in a positive, not negative, presentation. Cockiness will antagonize any board member and make him wonder if you are covering up a weakness by a false show of strength.

2) Get comfortable, but don't lounge or sprawl

Sit erectly but not stiffly. A careless posture may lead the board to conclude that you are careless in other things, or at least that you are not impressed by the importance of the occasion. Either conclusion is natural, even if incorrect. Do not fuss with your clothing, a pencil or an ashtray. Your hands may occasionally be useful to emphasize a point; do not let them become a point of distraction.

3) Do not wisecrack or make small talk

This is a serious situation, and your attitude should show that you consider it as such. Further, the time of the board is limited – they do not want to waste it, and neither should you.

4) Do not exaggerate your experience or abilities

In the first place, from information in the application or other interviews and sources, the board may know more about you than you think. Secondly, you probably will not get away with it. An experienced board is rather adept at spotting such a situation, so do not take the chance.

5) If you know a board member, do not make a point of it, yet do not hide it

Certainly you are not fooling him, and probably not the other members of the board. Do not try to take advantage of your acquaintanceship – it will probably do you little good.

6) Do not dominate the interview

Let the board do that. They will give you the clues – do not assume that you have to do all the talking. Realize that the board has a number of questions to ask you, and do not try to take up all the interview time by showing off your extensive knowledge of the answer to the first one.

7) Be attentive

You only have 20 minutes or so, and you should keep your attention at its sharpest throughout. When a member is addressing a problem or question to you, give him your undivided attention. Address your reply principally to him, but do not exclude the other board members.

8) Do not interrupt

A board member may be stating a problem for you to analyze. He will ask you a question when the time comes. Let him state the problem, and wait for the question.

9) Make sure you understand the question

Do not try to answer until you are sure what the question is. If it is not clear, restate it in your own words or ask the board member to clarify it for you. However, do not haggle about minor elements.

10) Reply promptly but not hastily

A common entry on oral board rating sheets is "candidate responded readily," or "candidate hesitated in replies." Respond as promptly and quickly as you can, but do not jump to a hasty, ill-considered answer.

11) Do not be peremptory in your answers

A brief answer is proper – but do not fire your answer back. That is a losing game from your point of view. The board member can probably ask questions much faster than you can answer them.

12) Do not try to create the answer you think the board member wants

He is interested in what kind of mind you have and how it works – not in playing games. Furthermore, he can usually spot this practice and will actually grade you down on it.

13) Do not switch sides in your reply merely to agree with a board member

Frequently, a member will take a contrary position merely to draw you out and to see if you are willing and able to defend your point of view. Do not start a debate, yet do not surrender a good position. If a position is worth taking, it is worth defending.

14) Do not be afraid to admit an error in judgment if you are shown to be wrong

The board knows that you are forced to reply without any opportunity for careful consideration. Your answer may be demonstrably wrong. If so, admit it and get on with the interview.

15) Do not dwell at length on your present job

The opening question may relate to your present assignment. Answer the question but do not go into an extended discussion. You are being examined for a *new* job, not your present one. As a matter of fact, try to phrase ALL your answers in terms of the job for which you are being examined.

Basis of Rating

Probably you will forget most of these "do's" and "don'ts" when you walk into the oral interview room. Even remembering them all will not ensure you a passing grade. Perhaps you did not have the qualifications in the first place. But remembering them will help you to put your best foot forward, without treading on the toes of the board members.

Rumor and popular opinion to the contrary notwithstanding, an oral board wants you to make the best appearance possible. They know you are under pressure – but they also want to see how you respond to it as a guide to what your reaction would be under the pressures of the job you seek. They will be influenced by the degree of poise you display, the personal traits you show and the manner in which you respond.

ABOUT THIS BOOK

This book contains tests divided into Examination Sections. Go through each test, answering every question in the margin. At the end of each test look at the answer key and check your answers. On the ones you got wrong, look at the right answer choice and learn. Do not fill in the answers first. Do not memorize the questions and answers, but understand the answer and principles involved. On your test, the questions will likely be different from the samples. Questions are changed and new ones added. If you understand these past questions you should have success with any changes that arise. Tests may consist of several types of questions. We have additional books on each subject should more study be advisable or necessary for you. Finally, the more you study, the better prepared you will be. This book is intended to be the last thing you study before you walk into the examination room. Prior study of relevant texts is also recommended. NLC publishes some of these in our Fundamental Series. Knowledge and good sense are important factors in passing your exam. Good luck also helps. So now study this Passbook, absorb the material contained within and take that knowledge into the examination. Then do your best to pass that exam.

EXAMINATION SECTION

EXAMINATION SECTION
TEST 1

DIRECTIONS: Each question or incomplete statement is followed by several suggested answers or completions. Select the one that BEST answers the question or completes the statement. *PRINT THE LETTER OF THE CORRECT ANSWER IN THE SPACE AT THE RIGHT.*

1. In the OSI model, the layer that is used to control how bit streams of data are sent and received over the physical medium is called
   A. application
   B. session
   C. transport
   D. physical
   1._____

2. Ergonomics is the
   A. cost relationship between computer hardware and software
   B. different computer operating systems
   C. human aspect of environment around the computer system
   D. gradation of various computer professionals
   2._____

3. The person who tries and gains illegal access to a computer network system is known as a(n)
   A. identify thief
   B. intruder
   C. cyber-terrorist
   D. hacker
   3._____

4. When encryption is adopted as a security procedure in the network, but it fails to protect the network from digital pests and hackers, which of the following methods should be adopted?
   A. Routers   B. Repeaters   C. Antivirus   D. Firewalls
   4._____

5. Comparison of processing speed between different computers are termed as
   A. CPS   B. MIPS   C. MPG   D. EFTS
   5._____

6. TSR stands for _____; they are loaded mostly in _____.
   A. test status request; config systems
   B. termination and stay resident program; autoexec.bat
   C. take status request; tsr.sys
   D. token set ready; msdos.sys
   6._____

7. Which of the following is NOT a typical component of a security program?
   A. The consequences for the person breaking the security policies
   B. The policies and protective measures that will be used
   C. The responsibilities of individuals involved in maintaining security
   D. The responsibilities of those who abide by established security policies
   7._____

8. The process of copying backed-up data back to the operational hard disk is called   8.____
    A. restoration
    B. back-up copy
    C. disaster recovery
    D. forward pass

9. Which one of the following is NOT a possible rule of thumb for backup and recovery?   9.____
    A. Back it up or give it up
    B. If it has not been backed up off-site, it will not survive a fire
    C. Tape rules – it's the only way to go for backup
    D. Ignored backup systems become poorly performing backup systems

10. Which command will display the assigned IP address of a network adapter installed on a Windows system?   10.____
    A. Ipadapter/all
    B. WinIP
    C. Ip config
    D. Configip

11. Which are examples of wireless encryption?   11.____
    A. Vpn and mac
    B. Ppp and mac
    C. weP and wpa
    D. VGA and USB

12. How do the network administrators make it possible to save the access to storage devices?   12.____
    A. By using zoning
    B. By putting a physical lock on the storage device
    C. By keeping devices shut down when not in use
    D. All of the above

13. Some analysts suggest that telecommuting will become more popular with managers and workers when   13.____
    A. workers are forced to telecommute
    B. managers finally give up the idea of controlling workers
    C. multimedia teleconferencing systems become affordable
    D. automobiles become outdated

14. Suppose you are the IT supervisor of a large company. You have to manage all of the Windows Server 2003 computers, client computers and printers. Network users are complaining that it is taking too much time for printing jobs from the network printer devices. These devices are high-speed printers and you have to determine whether the bottleneck is being caused by the network connection or by the print device itself. How can you track how much throughput is being processed by the print devices?   14.____
    A. Track the print object, bytes printed/sec counters in performance monitor
    B. Track the print queue object, bytes printed/sec counters in system monitor
    C. Track the print queue object, total pages printed/minute counters in performance monitor
    D. Track the print queue object, total pages printed/minute counter in system monitor

15. The U.S. government permits people legal access to the data collected   15.____
about them by government agencies through the
    A. Freedom of Information Act   B. Copyright Act of 1976
    C. Privacy Act of 1979   D. None of the above

16. Suppose you are working as the ISP help desk officer and you receive a   16.____
HELP call, using Outlook Express for sending and receiving e-mails but shifting
another computer of ICS feature enabled for sharing the Internet connection
with the old computer. After enabling ICS, he is not able to send or receive
emails. What will be the possible option to resolve this error?
    A. Recheck the "Always Use LAN Settings" option on Outlook Express under
       tools-accounts-mail properties section
    B. Use FQDN instead of just using mail account name
    C. ICS is only for sharing Internet connections so user cannot use emails
    D. Use Microsoft Outlook E and configure to a WINS server on LAN

17. Which computer activity is performed to track electronic or paper log?   17.____
    A. Traceroute   B. Cookie
    C. Web log   D. Audit trail

18. What is/are the limitations of the new IP Address Management tool in   18.____
Windows Server 2012?
    A. Only deals with servers that belong to designated Windows domains
    B. Centralized deployment is needed, which induces network latency
    C. It cannot manage DHCP appliances
    D. A and C

19. Which utility is useful in identifying a program that is hogging the processor?   19.____
    A. Task Manager   B. Device Manager
    C. System Monitor   D. System Information

20. A spell checker that checks every word as it is typed and beeps or flashes   20.____
each time a word is typed incorrectly is called
    A. idea processor   B. interactive spelling checking
    C. batch spelling checker   D. believability index

21. When the computer having a problem crashes ("blue screens"), for recovery   21.____
purpose making the copies of information in RAM, written to your boot partition
whenever the computer crashed, name copies of information as
    A. memory chunks   B. memory dumps
    C. files   D. folders

22. How do smart badges or active badges simultaneously improve security and threaten privacy?

    22.____

    A. A badge user's location can be monitored constantly
    B. Whenever anyone logs into a computer system, the badge's code identifies the person as an authorized or unauthorized user
    C. At the end of the day, it is possible to reconstruct a badge user's movement throughout the day
    D. All of the above

23. Jane has started an educational coaching center. To keep a record of students, a database has been developed. The database of students includes each student's parents' name and address, the student's date of birth, the course taken and current progress. Each month Jane sends every parent a personalized letter about the complete status of the student's progress, plus additional coaching required for each specific subject. The BEST way to personalize this mail would be to create

    23.____

    A. two word processor templates and cut and paste the appropriate details into each
    B. a starting document and use a conditional mail merge to insert the appropriate student information
    C. a database macro to extract each name from the database and merge it with the appropriate text
    D. a word processor macro to extract the student's name from the database and merge it with the suitable information

24. A small business organization wants to install a small-business server to save money for a separate investment on the Windows server and exchange server. But the owner never knows how many employees will be managed by the small business server. How many employees will be managed by the small business server?

    24.____

    A. 75   B. 200
    C. 500   D. Unlimited

25. Which is the biggest challenge for supervisors?

    25.____

    A. Working with a large team
    B. Dealing with a diversity of personalities
    C. Enjoying the best team work
    D. None of the above

KEY (CORRECT ANSWERS)

1.	D		11.	D
2.	C		12.	B
3.	D		13.	B
4.	D		14.	B
5.	B		15.	A
6.	B		16.	B
7.	A		17.	D
8.	A		18.	B
9.	D		19.	A
10.	C		20.	A

21.	B
22.	D
23.	D
24.	A
25.	B

TEST 2

DIRECTIONS: Each question or incomplete statement is followed by several suggested answers or completions. Select the one that BEST answers the question or completes the statement. *PRINT THE LETTER OF THE CORRECT ANSWER IN THE SPACE AT THE RIGHT.*

1.   FDDI is a _____ network.
    A. ring   B. star   C. mesh   D. bus

1.____

2.   What is the default administrative distance of an RIP protocol in a network?
    A. 110   B. 120   C. 30   D. 14   E. 151

2.____

3.   A measurement of network latency would be MOST helpful when troubleshooting problems associated with which service?
    A. E-mail   B. Web   C. VoIP   D. FTP

3.____

4.   You receive a call from a user saying that she has installed a new USB mouse on her Windows desktop. After installing the USB mouse, she restarted her desktop and the desktop crashes. You suspect that the problem is due to the USB mouse she installed. How do you restore the desktop to a workable state?
    A. Reinstall the OS
    B. Restart the desktop and press F8 during startup. The user should go to Safe mode and uninstall the driver.
    C. Use the last known good configuration
    D. Advise the user to remove the USB mouse

4.____

5.   As an IT supervisor, you receive a HELP call from one of the users. The complaint is that the computer seems very slow and keeps running out of disk space. What will be your suggestion for the user to get rid of unnecessary files and compress older files and keep the system active?
    A. Disk cleanup   B. Uninstall new updates
    C. File manager   D. Anti-virus

5.____

6.   VLOOKUP function purpose in MS Excel is to
    A. find the text that contains word 'v'
    B. check whether the text is the same in one cell as in the next
    C. find related records
    D. all of the above

6.____

7.   The acronym SILK (speech, image, language, and knowledge) is
    A. the name of a new desktop computer with futuristic capabilities
    B. one researcher's vision of the themes emerging in user interface technology
    C. the minimum qualification of a software agent
    D. a new type of multimedia software application

7.____

8. The portion of a program ignored by the computer since they are only
   included to help the reader understand the program is called
      A. variables   B. declarations
      C. reminder notes   D. comments

                                                                    8._____

Questions 9-10.

DIRECTIONS: Questions 9 and 10 are to be answered on the basis of the following case
study.

A public health center wants to create a database for its routine jobs like patient records,
operation schedules and storage classroom, as well as data storage back in the health care
center.

9. What does the organization require in regard to data loss and recovery plans?   9._____
   Organization must
      A. make and implement storage plans
      B. obtain insurance for destroyed and/or lost data
      C. develop lockdown procedures for data loss and critical business needs to
         be postponed
      D. establish a contingency plan with policies and procedures for responding
         to emergencies that block systems that contain electronic health records

10. In consideration for developing data backup, disaster recovery and emergency   10._____
    conditions for the health care center, what will be your suggestions?
       A. Documented agreement for organization is not enough. All procedures
          that the organization actually uses.
       B. Plans should be living documents, or rationalized on a regular basis with
          evolving requirements and methodologies
       C. Plans for each operation should be included, like hardware, software,
          responsible parties and potential vendors
       D. All of the above

11. How have data-related services changed over the past decade?   11._____
       A. Instead of online backup, firms are increasingly using a "duplicate and
          store" method to make and store a copy of organizational data
       B. Data management requirements are becoming more flexibly interpreted
       C. Local copies of data are now being purged from organizational storage
          and archived at a storage management firm
       D. None of the above

12. What should an organization NOT do when selecting a storage provider?   12.____
    A. Conduct a network analysis, required bandwidth and estimated travel
       times of data
    B. Look closely at service-level agreements
    C. Choose a company who is willing to accept all responsibility for data
       protection and security
    D. Look for effective methods to provide SLA faithfulness

13. How do organization mandates force change in small business backup   13.____
    strategies?
    A. Nudging businesses toward online backup policies, especially those with
       simple technology implementation
    B. Encouraging businesses to be as cost-effective as possible, as well as
       find ways to get the work completed
    C. Recognizing the importance of backing up data for the organizations
    D. All of the above

14. Outlook Express can acknowledge connections of the server from which of   14.____
    the following servers?
    A. Mailbox   B. Client Access
    C. Unified Messaging   D. Hub Transport

15. Why do many companies use callback security systems in which the   15.____
    computer calls the user on the phone before allowing access?
    A. To identify user by voice recognition
    B. To check the phone line for modern taps
    C. To prevent unauthorized user stolen passwords
    D. Actually, callback systems are outdated

16. The form of computer-assisted instruction known as drill and practice   16.____
    A. helps the user learn to think in ways that are not possible otherwise
    B. does not help the user learn to think but helps user memorize the facts
       and skills
    C. does not help students learn to think better or to memorize facts and
       skills; in fact, it is nearly worthless
    D. allows student to program computers with easy to understand language

17. Suppose your company wants to send an advertising flyer to all State of New York   17.____
    residents with at least 5 acres of property. To select the appropriate records
    from the database, which select rules should you use?
    State EQUALS New York
    A. AND acreages GREATER THAN 5
    B. OR acreages GREATER THAN 5
    C. OR acreages GREATER THAN OR EQUAL TO 5
    D. AND acreages GREATER THAN OR EQUAL TO 5

18. As an IT supervisor you receive a HELP call from the user. The issue is that the user cannot access the shared accounts database files. Which is the MOST appropriate response?

    A. "Restart your computer."
    B. "Can you identify yourself and clarify the problem?"
    C. "I'm busy on another task; remind me in half an hour if probe is still there."
    D. "Network technician will be sent to you as soon as available to check the cabling on your PC."

18.____

19. John wants to scan a document to apply for a job online. He does not know how to scan. Which type of documentation will help him?

    A. User manual
    B. Drivers booklet
    C. Technical reference manual
    D. Installation manual

19.____

20. Which layer in an OSI model defines the formats the data uses as it is transmitted on the communication line?

    A. Application
    B. Physical
    C. Presentation
    D. Transport

20.____

21. Which is the situation in which organizations enforce separation of duties?

    A. Observance according to federal union rules
    B. Validation that all employees know their job tasks
    C. Improvement for a better work environment
    D. Considered valuable in deterring fraud

21.____

22. What will be the last step in changing the control process for any organization?

    A. Testing and implementation
    B. Review and improvement
    C. System validated and approved
    D. Report change to management

22.____

23. To evaluate the security of large networks, which one of the following strategies is MOST efficient?

    A. Monitor the login errors and interview the network manager
    B. Survey the network managers and interview all the users
    C. Observe the login errors and interview all the network users
    D. Survey the company manager and monitor all network users

23.____

24. When making decisions for the upgrade of information systems, the manager chooses the software specifically written for the organization. Writing the new software program occurs in which phase of the system development life cycle?

    A. Design
    B. Evaluation
    C. Development
    D. Implementation

24.____

25. Kim has created some official documents on her home computer due to
additional work load. When she opened those files on the official network
computer, they appeared in a different font. Why did this happen?   25._____
    A. She had a different printer at the office than at home
    B. She has a different monitor at the office than at home
    C. The font she used at home is not installed on her office computer
    D. The version of Windows is different

KEY (CORRECT ANSWERS)

1.	A		11.	D
2.	B		12.	C
3.	C		13.	D
4.	B		14.	B
5.	A		15.	C
6.	C		16.	B
7.	D		17.	D
8.	D		18.	B
9.	D		19.	A
10.	D		20.	B

21.	D
22.	D
23.	A
24.	C
25.	C

TEST 3

DIRECTIONS: Each question or incomplete statement is followed by several suggested answers or completions. Select the one that BEST answers the question or completes the statement. *PRINT THE LETTER OF THE CORRECT ANSWER IN THE SPACE AT THE RIGHT.*

1. A terminal is a
    A. device to give power supply to a computer
    B. point at which data enters or leaves the computer
    C. the last instructor in a program
    D. any input or output

1.____

2. How many TCP ports are used by SMTP?
    A. 42   B. 33   C. 27   D. 25

2.____

3. Which Internet program is used to validate that a particular Internet address exists and can accept requests?
    A. URL   B. Ping
    C. Noc   D. Bandwidth test

3.____

4. Can we run Windows Server 2012 systems in a cluster with previous versions of Windows Server?
    A. Yes   B. No

4.____

5. Connectivity issues of LAN on router can be checked with one of these commands:
    I.   Show interfaces   II. Show IP route
    III. Tracert   IV. Ping
    V.   Dns

    The CORRECT answer is:
    A. I, II, IV   B. III and V
    C. None of the above   D. All of the above

5.____

6. Which is the protocol to control data backup and recovery and also communicate between the primary and secondary storage in a heterogeneous network environment?
    A. NDMP (Network Data Management Protocol)
    B. Network Data Management
    C. TCP/IP (Transmission Control Protocol/Internet Protocol)
    D. None of the above

6.____

7. Data backup devices like rewritable and erasable (CD-R/W) optical disk require short time storage for changeable data but require
    A. faster file access than tape   B. slower file access than tape
    C. slower file access than drive   D. slower file access than scale

7.____

8. As an IT supervisor, you receive a HELP call. The user is constantly
receiving a large amount of attached spam emails and needs to rectify this
issue immediately. What is the BEST option to eliminate this problem?
    A. Restart the SMTP/POP3 mail services
    B. Check the incoming mails in the mail queue, find out the source address,
       and block them accordingly
    C. Utilize the antivirus, spam control and content filtering applications on the
       mail servers and do not allow unacceptable messages through the mail
       gateway
    D. The mail relay agent should be configured properly

8._____

9. A management information system (MIS) can be used by
    A. only top level managers in the company
    B. only mind level managers in the company
    C. only low level managers in the company
    D. one MIS can be used by all levels of management

9._____

10. The following aspects of the writing processes can be at least partially
computerized with widely available commercial software EXCEPT
    A. organizing plan
    B. producing an index
    C. checking holes in the plot of a novel
    D. checking for grammatical errors

10._____

11. Which of the following is NOT true regarding CAM?
    A. It is used in inflexible manufacturing
    B. It improves the overall efficiency of the manufacturing process
    C. It reduces the time needed to set up machines or robots for the next
       production run
    D. It makes it possible to accompany a response to a customer's unique
       needs

11._____

12. Companies use call-back security systems in which the computer calls the user
on the phone before allowing access in order to
    A. initialize voice-recognition programs
    B. clear the line for better call quality
    C. prevent unauthorized use of stolen passwords
    D. record the conversation for review purposes

12._____

13. Bayesian algorithms are used in a majority of spam filters that keep a record
of all incoming e-mails. Like other characteristics, it determines the e-mail
message as spam. Bayesian algorithms logic is based on
    A. set theory probability   B. game theory
    C. number theory   D. probability

13._____

14. As a network officer, you are on a HELP call. The complaint is that the user thinks that someone is logging into her computer after she leaves her desk at work. Which tool would you use to track who logs on and off the computer?
    A. Log monitor snap-in
    B. System monitors
    C. Task Manager
    D. Performance logs and Alert snaps in

14.____

15. In an OSI model, data link layer has two separate sub layers which are
    A. LLC and MAC
    B. CS and MA
    C. Token and Ring
    D. Ethernet

15.____

16. According to Alan Kay's four rules for predicting the future, how long does it take for new technology to go from the research lab to the marketplace?
    A. Six months
    B. Three years
    C. Ten years
    D. A generation

16.____

17. As a help desk officer, you are on a HELP call from one of the users. While troubleshooting, the computer needs to reboot several times. For every reboot, the log-on screen appears and prompts you for a username and password before you can continue working. The concerned user has been in a meeting. How do you proceed?
    A. Call user, ask for password, type it in, and continue with troubleshooting
    B. Insist user stay there and have him type the password each time when needed
    C. Call user, ask him to come to type password every time when needed
    D. Request user temporarily change his password until you have completed your work

17.____

18. One of the world's largest multinational companies has managers located around the world in France, China, Japan and Australia. Which decision-making technique seems BEST suited for this organization?
    A. Postal-service interaction
    B. Brainstorming session
    C. Nominal discussion
    D. Electronic meeting

18.____

19. As an IT supervisor, you receive a troubleshooting call. The problem is in connecting to the hard drive controller of Windows 7 system due to the older, unsigned driver. What can you do to make Windows a load driver?
    A. Start the computer in Disable Drive Signature Enforcement mode
    B. Install the driver in Windows XP compatibility mode
    C. It is impossible
    D. In Device Manager, use the Legacy Driver option

19.____

20. There has been a deduction of an employee's one-day salary due to his uninformed leave. He was already warned about this behavior. This is an example of which method of shaping behaviors?
    A. Reinforcement
    B. Positive reinforcement
    C. Punishment
    D. Negative reinforcement

20.____

13

21. Which of the following are three essential skills that supervisors need to have in order to achieve their objectives?
    A. Technical, decisional and interpersonal
    B. Technical, human and conceptual
    C. Interpersonal, informational and decisional
    D. Conceptual, communication and networking

    21.____

22. Expansion slots connecting interfaces are
    A. ports
    B. peripheral devices
    C. motherboard
    D. system bus

    22.____

23.

Straight-through cable

IP Address: 192.168.1.20
Mask   : 255.255.255.240

IP Address : 192.168.1.201
Mask   : 255.255.255.240

    23.____

As a network technician, when you are connecting two hosts, computer A and computer B, directly through their Ethernet interfaces, Ping attempt is not working between these two hosts. How will you connect these two hosts?
I .   A crossover cable should be used
II.   A rollover cable should be used
III. The subnet masks should be set to 255.255.255.192
IV.   A default gateway needs to be set on each host
V.   The subnet masks should be set to 255.255.255.0

    23.____

The CORRECT answer is:
    A. I only
    B. II only
    C. III and IV only
    D. I and V only
    E. II and V only

24. On a network, the act of listening to the medium for a message is called
    A. contention
    B. carrier sensing
    C. collision
    D. transparency

    24.____

25. As the network administrator, you are continuously having network performance issues and you want to improve the performance by increasing the bandwidth available to hosts and limiting the size of broadband options. What will be your choice for your network?
    A. Managed hubs
    B. Switches
    C. Bridges
    D. Switches configured with VLAN's

    25.____

KEY (CORRECT ANSWERS)

1.	B	11.	A
2.	D	12.	C
3.	B	13.	D
4.	B	14.	D
5.	A	15.	A
6.	A	16.	C
7.	A	17.	D
8.	C	18.	D
9.	D	19.	A
10.	C	20.	C

21.	B
22.	C
23.	D
24.	B
25.	D

———

TEST 4

DIRECTIONS: Each question or incomplete statement is followed by several suggested answers or completions. Select the one that BEST answers the question or completes the statement. *PRINT THE LETTER OF THE CORRECT ANSWER IN THE SPACE AT THE RIGHT.*

1. A stand-alone computer can be a
   A. computer not connected to the network
   B. portable computer
   C. computer connected to the network
   D. keyboard or mouse

   1.____

2. Which problem occurs when two workstations on a shared Ethernet are trying to access LAN at the same time?
   A. Local talk   B. Deadlock
   C. Collision   D. Concession

   2.____

3. In designing a network, the number of hubs and switches are determined by the number of computers that will be attached to this network.
   A. True   B. False

   3.____

4. Which type of data transmission uses a clock to control the timing of bits being sent?
   A. Synchronous   B. Asynchronous
   C. Parallel   D. None of the above

   4.____

5. Which point acts as an entrance to another network? On the Internet, a node or stopping point can be either one of these nodes or a host (end-point) node.
   A. Gateway   B. Routers   C. Repeater

   5.____

6. The time taken by a data signal to reach the moon and then back to earth is about two _____.
   A. minutes   B. seconds
   C. milliseconds   D. hours

   6.____

7. As an IT supervisor, you receive a HELP call from a user unable to save a file that he is currently updating on a shared directory. While attempting to save the file, the error message is displayed: "This file is locked for editing by another user." This type of issue is categorized as
   A. bug in the program   B. access rights
   C. connectivity   D. security

   7.____

8. Managers can use _____ to help with planning, staffing, directing and controlling organization, but can suffer the possibility of _____.
   A. virtual reality; algorithm overload
   B. database management systems; de-skilling
   C. computer monitoring; de-skilling
   D. management information systems; information overload

   8.____

9. Every organization has a disaster recovery plan. Which of the following is   9._____
   NOT a good choice for DRP (Disaster Recovery Plan)?
   A. Define unacceptable every loss   B. Check on server speed
   C. Mange all   D. Document what you have done

10. One way a database manager might be able to see if an intruder has been   10._____
    on the system is by using
    A. an encryption device   B. audit control software
    C. a copy protection scheme   D. a password

11. In your new job as a widget company statistician, you have asked 500 of   11._____
    your customers to fill out a survey that includes questions about the
    educational level, income and number of widgets purchased annually. After
    you enter the data in a spreadsheet program, you decide to look for a
    relationship between income and the number of widgets purchased. The BEST
    way to display the data for this kind of speculation is a _____ chart.
    A. bullet   B. line   C. pie   D. scatter

12. Which of the following commands changes any or all of the target words to a   12._____
    different word and comes in handy when you have misspelled the same words
    or name throughout your document?
    A. Replace command   B. Edit command
    C. Cut and replace command   D. None of the above

13. John is running a club. He is trying to decide how much to charge for dues for   13._____
    each club member, but he cannot figure out how his cost stacks up against
    some best case or worst case sale projections. What is he going to use for this
    purpose?
    A. Word processor   B. Outliner
    C. Spreadsheet   D. Idea process

14. When users view and change values interactively while using a database, the   14._____
    process is referred to as
    A. batching   B. real time
    C. high speed   D. just in time

15. NOW () function returns the   15._____
    A. current date and time
    B. serial number of current time
    C. serial number of the current date
    D. none of the above

16. The oldest spreadsheet package is   16._____
    A. VisiCalc   B. Lotus 1-2-3
    C. Excel   D. Star Calc

17. The ability of word processing software to combine name and address with a standard document is called
    A. address book
    B. mail merge
    C. document formatting
    D. letter formatting

17.____

18. As a help desk officer, you receive a HELP call from one of the users, who had a printing troubleshooting problem at his end. The user explains in detail exactly what he was trying to do and what happened with the printer when he gave the print command. He tried to diagnose the problem and either wrong names or paper jam. At what point should you interrupt him?
    A. After he describes the first problem
    B. As soon as you understand the problem
    C. As soon as you have a solution
    D. Never

18.____

19. A password with all possible combinations of numbers and characters is considered a more difficult one. This type of password recovery is quite difficult and is called
    A. passive
    B. active
    C. dictionary
    D. brute force

19.____

20. A uniform change is placed _____ on the photosensitive drum during the laser printer's conditioning phase.
    A. +1000 volt
    B. +600 volts
    C. -600 volts
    D. -1000 volts
    E. +12 volts

20.____

21.

In the above shown image, which will be the CORRECT example of firewall placement in the organization's network?
    A. First Option
    B. Second option
    C. Third option
    D. Fourth option
    E. None of the above

21.____

22. When a hard disk has gone old, it loses its ability to store information. This   22._____
slow loss can be defined as
    A. corrupted frequently sectors   B. bad sectors
    C. fatal errors to frequent   D. corrupted partition tables

23. A small organizational management is worried about their staff who   23._____
accidentally introduces computer viruses into their network system. What
would you suggest to the BEST of your knowledge as the IT supervisor?
    A. Allow the users to download music files to put onto their MP3 players
    B. Give the free hand to users to attach flash/pen drives using the USB
       connection
    C. Install the latest anti-virus software on all their computers
    D. Do not have an acceptable use policy

24. When working in large organizations, you have to face different situations.   24._____
For example, whenever you come back from lunch or reach the office late, your
manager never gives you the benefit of the doubt. He assumes that you had
simply wasted too much time. He never considers that the elevators were out
and you had to walk up ten flights of stairs or you are stuck in a traffic jam.
What do you think your boss is guilty of?
    A. Self-serving bias   B. Selective perception
    C. Fundamental attribution error   D. Inconsistency

25. In large organizations, people come up with different opinions. For example,   25._____
when two people see the situation at the same time yet interpret it differently.
Which factors operate to shape their dissimilar perceptions?
    A. Perceivers   B. Target
    C. Timing   D. Context

KEY (CORRECT ANSWERS)

1.	A		11.	D
2.	C		12.	A
3.	A		13.	C
4.	A		14.	B
5.	A		15.	D
6.	B		16.	A
7.	B		17.	B
8.	D		18.	D
9.	B		19.	D
10.	B		20.	C

21.	A
22.	B
23.	C
24.	C
25.	A

EXAMINATION SECTION
TEST 1

DIRECTIONS: Each question or incomplete statement is followed by several suggested answers or completions. Select the one that BEST answers the question or completes the statement. *PRINT THE LETTER OF THE CORRECT ANSWER IN THE SPACE AT THE RIGHT.*

1. The stage in a system's life cycle in which logical and physical specifications are pro-   1._____
   duced is called

   A. implementation   B. design
   C. conception   D. documentation

2. Which of the following is a network topology that links a number of computers by a single   2._____
   circuit with all messages broadcast to the entire network?

   A. Daisy–chain   B. Broadband
   C. Bus   D. Ring

3. Of the following statements about information as a resource, which is generally FALSE?   3._____

   A. It has value and lends itself to the process of management.
   B. It can be overabundant and overused.
   C. Its usefulness tends to decrease with time.
   D. It can be consumed and expended in the same way as many capital resources.

4. What is the term for the extra bit built into EBCDIC and ASCII codes that is used as a   4._____
   check bit to insure accuracy?

   A. Parity   B. Auditor   C. Damper   D. Buffer

5. In the systems development process, which of the following is typically performed   5._____
   FIRST?

   A. Conversion   B. Programming
   C. Production   D. Testing

6. Which of the following is a term for a device used to store and retrieve large numbers of   6._____
   optical disks?

   A. Warehouse   B. Vault   C. Clearing   D. Jukebox

7. Each of the following can generally be said to be an element of the changing contempo-   7._____
   rary business environment EXCEPT

   A. global work groups   B. stable environment
   C. location independence   D. time–based competition

8. Of the following methods of changing from one information system to another, which is   8._____
   generally considered to be the safest?

   A. Pilot study   B. Direct cutover
   C. Phased approach   D. Parallel strategy

9. Which of the following is NOT typically a characteristic of a management information system?   9.___

   A. Extensive analytical capability
   B. Known and stable information requirements
   C. Internal rather than external orientation
   D. Generally reporting–and control–oriented

10. In information systems terminology, a person, place, or thing about which information must be kept is referred to as a(n)   10.___

   A. element   B. entity
   C. assemblage   D. pixel

11. Which of the following are considered to be moral dimensions that are emblematic of the information age?   11.___
      I.   Accountability and control
      II.   Property rights
      III. Quality of life
      IV.   Information rights and obligations
   The CORRECT answer is:

   A. I, II   B. I, II, III
   C. I, III, IV   D. I, II, III, IV

12. In order to be classified as a *mainframe,* a computer must typically have at LEAST   12.___

   A. 1 remote access server
   B. 50 megabytes of RAM
   C. 1 gigabyte of RAM
   D. 5 gigabytes of secondary storage space

13. For most organizations, the FIRST step in developing a telecommunications plan should be to   13.___

   A. identify critical areas where telecommunications currently has an impact
   B. identify the organization's long–range business plan
   C. identify critical areas where telecommunications may have a future impact
   D. audit existing telecommunications functions

14. What is the term for a change in a data signal, from positive to negative or vice–versa, that is used as a measure of transmission speed?   14.___

   A. Baud   B. Switch   C. Byte   D. Bit

15. Currently, in service industries such as finance, insurance, and real estate, information technology generally constitutes about _____% of invested capital.   15.___

   A. 10   B. 30   C. 50   D. 70

16. Which of the following signifies the emerging standard language for relational database management systems?   16.___

   A. SGML   B. HTML   C. Perl   D. SQL

17. Over time, organizations have developed an ethical framework for handling system—related issues. Generally, the first step in any organization's ethical analysis should be to identify

    A. the higher—order values involved
    B. the potential consequences of any decision
    C. reasonable options
    D. the stakeholders

17.____

18. Telephone lines that are continously available for transmission by a lessee are described as

    A. validated   B. denuded
    C. formalized   D. dedicated

18.____

19. In a typical telecommunications system, a message that originates from the host computer will then pass through a

    A. front—end processor   B. modem
    C. controller   D. multiplexer

19.____

20. The table or list that relates record keys to physical locations on direct access files is called the

    A. key   B. index   C. card file   D. criterion

20.____

21. Which of the following offers the best definition of *data* as it applies to information systems?

    A. Things that are known to have occurred, to exist, or to be true
    B. Productions of exact copies of documents by electronic scanning and transmission
    C. Information not previously known to people within an organization
    D. Raw facts that have not been organized and arranged into understandable and usable form

21.____

22. A logical unit of a program that performs one or a small number of functions is known as a(n)

    A. module   B. element   C. loop   D. packet

22.____

23. Which of the following is a fourth—generation computer language?

    A. FORTRAN   B. dBASE   C. C   D. Ada

23.____

24. The logical description of an entire database, listing all the data elements and the relationships among them, is known as the

    A. value chain   B. schema
    C. matrix   D. shell

24.____

25. Systems theory defines a system as an entity that is generally greater than the sum of its parts. Which of the following terms describes this condition?

    A. Synchronicity   B. Collectivism
    C. Interdependence D. Synergy

25.____

KEY (CORRECT ANSWERS)

1.	B		11.	D
2.	C		12.	B
3.	D		13.	D
4.	A		14.	A
5.	D		15.	D
6.	D		16.	D
7.	B		17.	A
8.	D		18.	D
9.	A		19.	A
10.	B		20.	B

21.	D
22.	A
23.	B
24.	B
25.	D

——————

TEST 2

DIRECTIONS: Each question or incomplete statement is followed by several suggested answers or completions. Select the one that BEST answers the question or completes the statement. *PRINT THE LETTER OF THE CORRECT ANSWER IN THE SPACE AT THE RIGHT.*

1. Of the types of organizational change that are enabled by information technology, which involves the highest levels of risk and reward?   1.____

    A.   Paradigm shift
    B.   Automation
    C.   Business reengineering
    D.   Rationalization of procedures

2. Most local–area networks (LANS) are _____ networks.   2.____

    A.   token ring   B.   ring   C.   star   D.   bus

3. Which of the following is an input device which translates images into digital form for processing?   3.____

    A.   Surveyor   B.   Pen   C.   Compiler   D.   Scanner

4. In a system, the appearance of an additional pattern or sequence of states is referred to as   4.____

    A.   autonomy   B.   differentiation
    C.   bifurcation   D.   variation

5. Which of the following is NOT considered to be an information output?   5.____

    A.   Storage   B.   Expert–system advice
    C.   Query response   D.   Report

6. Which of the following is a direct access storage device (DASD)?   6.____

    A.   Punch card   B.   Sequential tape
    C.   Printed page   D.   Magnetic disk

7. Which of the following is most likely to be an output from a knowledge work system (KWS)?   7.____

    A.   Special report   B.   Model
    C.   Summary report   D.   Query response

8. A system resting on accepted and fixed definitions of data and procedures, operating with predefined rules, is described in systems terminology as   8.____

    A.   formal   B.   computer–based
    C.   fixed   D.   expert

9. Which of the following is a characteristic of operational data?
They   9.____

    A.   are stored on a single platform
    B.   contain recent as well as historical data
    C.   are organized around major business informational subjects
    D.   are generally used by isolated legacy systems

10. Which of the following signifies a telecommunications network that requires its own dedicated channels and encompasses a limited physical distance?

    A. WAN   B. KWS   C. LAN   D. ISDN

10.__

11. Which of the following terms is used for the capture or collection of raw data from within the organization, or from its external environment, for processing in an information system?

    A. Feedback   B. Tracking   C. Entry   D. Input

11.__

12. What is the term for the high–speed storage of frequently used instructions and data?

    A. Cache   B. Index   C. Reserve   D. Packet

12.__

13. Which of the following represents the largest unit of data?

    A. Byte   B. Record   C. Field   D. File

13.__

14. In most organizations, the entire system–building effort is driven by

    A. user information requirements
    B. existing hardware
    C. user training requirements
    D. availability of packaged applications

14.__

15. Which of the following terms is used to describe a process of change governed by probabilities at each step?

    A. Adiabatic   B. Stochastic
    C. Multifinal   D. Probabilistic

15.__

16. In object–oriented programming, a specific class of objects often receives the features of a more general class. This process is referred to as

    A. aliasing   B. inheritance
    C. summation   D. incrementation

16.__

17. In a typical organization, the strategic planning of an MIS would be the responsibility of the

    A. steering committee
    B. project teams
    C. operations personnel and end users
    D. chief information officer

17.__

18. Which of the following is a specialized computer that supervises communications traffic between the CPU and the peripheral devices in a telecommunications system?

    A. Controller   B. Concentrator
    C. Connector   D. Compiler

18.__

19. Of the following steps in the machine cycle of a computer, which occurs FIRST?   19._____

    A. Transmission of data from main memory to storage register
    B. Placement of instruction in instruction register
    C. ALU performance
    D. Placement of instruction in address register

20. Which of the following is a process of recoding information which reduces the number of   20._____
different characters in a message while increasing the different number of characters to
be recognized?

    A. The black box method   B. Daisy chaining
    C. Aliasing   D. Chunking

21. Of the following methodologies for establishing organizational MIS requirements, which   21._____
is most explicitly oriented toward deploying information systems as a competitive
weapon?

    A. Critical success factors (CSF)
    B. Strategic cube and value chain
    C. Business sytems planning (BSP)
    D. Strategy set transformation

22. Which of the following is a type of MIS application used for tracking and monitoring?   22._____

    A. Database
    B. Decision Support System (DSS)
    C. Spreadsheet
    D. Desktop publishing

23. An organization's information requirements are often analyzed by looking at the entire   23._____
organization in terms of units, functions, processes, and data elements. What is the term
most frequently used for such an examination?

    A. Semantic networking   B. Decision support
    C. Enterprise analysis   D. Run control

24. Which of the following would most likely be classifed as an *information worker*?   24._____

    A. Engineer   B. Scientist
    C. Data processor   D. Architect

25. In an organization that uses a decision support system to make stock investment deci-   25._____
sions, which of the following would be classified as memory aids to the system?

    A. Graphs   B. Databases
    C. Menus   D. Training documents

———

KEY (CORRECT ANSWERS)

1.	A	11.	D
2.	D	12.	A
3.	D	13.	D
4.	C	14.	A
5.	A	15.	B
6.	D	16.	B
7.	B	17.	D
8.	A	18.	A
9.	D	19.	B
10.	C	20.	D

21.	B
22.	A
23.	C
24.	C
25.	B

TEST 3

DIRECTIONS: Each question or incomplete statement is followed by several suggested answers or completions. Select the one that BEST answers the question or completes the statement. *PRINT THE LETTER OF THE CORRECT ANSWER IN THE SPACE AT THE RIGHT.*

1. In the _____ process, the components of a system and their relationship to each other are laid out as they would appear to users. 1.____

    A. external integration   B. logical design
    C. file serving   D. hierarchical

2. Over the past two decades, technological trends have raised ethical issues in society, especially in the area of privacy. Which of the following trends has LEAST directly impacted the issue of privacy? 2.____

    A. Advances in data storage techniques and declining storage costs
    B. Advances in telecommunications infrastructure
    C. The doubling of computer power every 18 months
    D. Advances in data mining techniques for large databases

3. Which of the following systems exists at the strategic level of an organization? 3.____

    A. Expert system
    B. Decision support system (DSS)
    C. Value chain
    D. Executive support system (ESS)

4. Which of the following is equal to one–billionth of a second? 4.____

    A. Millisecond   B. Picosecond
    C. Nanosecond   D. Microsecond

5. A small section of a program that can be easily stored in primary storage and quickly accessed from secondary storage is a(n) 5.____

    A. sector   B. module   C. page   D. applet

6. Which of the following statements about hierarchical and network database systems is TRUE? 6.____
They

    A. do support English–language inquiries for information
    B. involve easily changeable access pathways
    C. are difficult to install
    D. are relatively inefficient processors

7. Which of the following is a programming language that is portable across different brands of soft hardware, and is used for both military and nonmilitary applications? 7.____

    A. FORTRAN   B. Pascal   C. Ada   D. C

8. Which of the following would be LEAST likely to be an output of an office automation system (OAS)? 8.____

    A. Memo   B. Schedule   C. List   D. Mail

9. At a minimum, an information system must consist of all of the following EXCEPT 9.___

   A. computers   B. data   C. people   D. procedures

10. What is the term for the strategy used to search through the rule base in an expert system? 10.___

   A. Index server   B. Key field
   C. Register   D. Inference engine

11. Which of the following communications media has the greatest frequency range? 11.___

   A. Wireless (electromagnetic)
   B. Fiber optics
   C. Wireless (PCS)
   D. Microwave

12. Models of decision–making in which decisions are shaped by the organization's standard operation procedures are described as 12.___

   A. systems–oriented   B. indexed
   C. bureaucratic   D. sequential

13. The first element involved in a standard dataflow diagram is a(n) 13.___

   A. dataflow   B. external entity
   C. data store   D. process

14. A system that seeks a set of related goals is described as 14.___

   A. purposive   B. closed   C. fixed   D. driven

15. Weaknesses in a system's _____ controls may affect the entire system of general controls, which may not be properly executed or enforced. 15.___

   A. administrative   B. software
   C. implementation   D. computer operations

16. Current and historical data from operational systems is often consolidated for management reporting and analysis into a database with reporting and query tools. This type of database is usually referred to as a(n) 16.___

   A. warehouse   B. redundancy
   C. controller   D. library

17. A project manager at an organization plans to compose letters outlining details of an upcoming trade show to be addressed individually to several dozen employees. The most appropriate type of application for this purpose is 17.___

   A. simple word processing   B. desktop publishing
   C. a mail merge   D. an automated document

18. In the process of systems analysis, which of the following procedures is typically per-   18.____
    formed FIRST?

    A. Defining a problem that can be solved by a newly designed system
    B. Examining existing documents
    C. Identifying the primary owners and users of data in the organization
    D. Identifying the information requirements that must be met by a system solution

19. Each of the following is a method for performing a data quality audit EXCEPT surveying   19.____

    A. data dictionaries
    B. entire data files
    C. end users for perceptions of data quality
    D. samples from data files

20. Which of the following signifies semiconductor memory chips that contain program   20.____
    instructions?

    A. RAM   B. ROM   C. CPU   D. ALU

21. The Fair Information Practices Principles set forth in 1973 include: 21.____
    I.   Individuals have rights of access, inspection, review, and amendment to sys-
         tems that contain information about them
    II. Managers of systems are responsible and can be held liable for the damages
         done by systems, for the reliability, and for their security
    III. Managers do not have the right of access to any form of interorganizational
         correspondence if individuals do not wish to grant such access
    IV. Governments have the right to intervene in the information relationships
         among private parties
    The CORRECT answer is:

    A. I, II   B. II, III
    C. I, II, IV   D. II, III, IV

22. In information systems terminology, a group of records of the same type is known as a   22.____

    A. class   B. field   C. batch   D. file

23. In systems theory, communication which travels through informal rather than formal   23.____
    channels is known as

    A. noise
    B. back channel communication
    C. cross–talk
    D. the grapevine

24. In order to be useful as a resource, information must satisfy each of the following condi-   24.____
    tions EXCEPT it must

    A. be accurate
    B. be available when needed
    C. reinforce beliefs
    D. relate to the business or matters at hand

25. In most contemporary organizations, the role of an MIS department can be described as   25.___

   A. performing key design and analysis functions, before and after a systems design has been implemented
   B. designing, installing, testing, and maintaining all organizational computer–based information and communications systems
   C. providing and perfecting all information and communications needs at the organization's management level
   D. coordinating corporate MIS efforts and providing an overall computational infra-structure

---

KEY (CORRECT ANSWERS)

1.	B	11.	C
2.	C	12.	C
3.	D	13.	B
4.	C	14.	A
5.	C	15.	A
6.	C	16.	A
7.	C	17.	C
8.	C	18.	C
9.	A	19.	A
10.	D	20.	B

21.	C
22.	D
23.	B
24.	C
25.	D

EXAMINATION SECTION
TEST 1

DIRECTIONS: Each question or incomplete statement is followed by several suggested answers or completions. Select the one that BEST answers the question or completes the statement. *PRINT THE LETTER OF THE CORRECT ANSWER IN THE SPACE AT THE RIGHT.*

1. Representations of human knowledge used in expert systems generally include each of the following EXCEPT

    A. frames
    B. semantic nets
    C. fuzzy logic
    D. rules

1.____

2. Routines performed to verify input data and correct errors prior to processing are known as

    A. edit checks
    B. pilots
    C. control aids
    D. data audits

2.____

3. Which of the following statements about database management systems is generally FALSE?
They

    A. are able to separate logical and physical views of data
    B. eliminate data confusion by providing central control of data creation and definitions
    C. reduce data redundancy
    D. involve slight increases in program development and maintenance costs

3.____

4. In systems theory, there is a *what-if* method of treating uncertainty that explores the effect on the alternatives of environmental change. This method is generally referred to as _____ analysis.

    A. sensitivity
    B. contingency
    C. a fortiori
    D. systems

4.____

5. One of the core capabilities of a decision support system (DSS) is the logical and mathematical manipulation of data_____ a capability referred to as

    A. control aids
    B. representations
    C. memory aids
    D. operations

5.____

6. What is the term for the ability to move software from one generation of hardware to another more powerful generation?

    A. Adaptability
    B. Interoperability
    C. Multitasking
    D. Migration

6.____

7. In an enterprise information system, which of the following is considered to be an input control?

    A. Documentation of operating procedures
    B. Reviews of processing logs
    C. Verification of control totals
    D. Program testing

7.____

8. Low-speed transmission of data that occurs one character at a time is described as   8.___

    A. asynchronous   B. unchained
    C. phased   D. unstructured

9. Which of the following is a disadvantage associated with the use of relational databases?   9.___

    A. Limited ability to combine information from different sources
    B. Simplicity in maintenance
    C. Relatively slower speed of operation
    D. Limited flexibility regarding ad hoc queries

10. When all the elements in a system are in the same category, _____ is said to be at a   10.___
minimum.

    A. uncertainty   B. synergy
    C. inefficiency   D. entropy

11. Which of the following is most likely to rely on parallel processing?   11.___

    A. Minicomputer   B. Workstation
    C. Microcomputer   D. Supercomputer

12. In imaging systems, what is the term for the device that allows a user to identify and   12.___
retrieve a specific document?

    A. Forward chain   B. Index server
    C. Knowledge base   D. Search engine

13. Which of the following systems exists at the strategic level of an organization?   13.___

    A. Decision support system (DSS)
    B. Executive support system (ESS)
    C. Knowledge work system (KWS)
    D. Management information system (MIS)

14. What is the term for the secondary storage device on which a complete operating system   14.___
is stored?

    A. Central Processing Unit   B. Microprocessor
    C. Optical code recognizer   D. System residence drive

15. Which of the following is NOT a type of knowledge work system (KWS)?   15.___

    A. Investment workstations
    B. Virtual reality systems
    C. Computer-aided design (CAD)
    D. Decision support system (DSS)

16. A transmission over a telecommunications network in which data can flow two ways, but   16.___
in only one direction at a time, is described as

    A. simplex   B. half duplex
    C. full duplex   D. multiplex

17. The functions of knowledge workers in an organization generally include each of the following EXCEPT

    A. updating knowledge
    B. managing documentation of knowledge
    C. serving as internal consultants
    D. acting as change agents

17.____

18. The predominant programming language for business was

    A. Perl   B. COBOL   C. FORTRAN   D. SGML

18.____

19. In general, the technology associated with reduced instruction set (RISC) computers is most appropriate for

    A. decision support systems (DSS)
    B. network communications
    C. scientific and workstation computing
    D. desktop publishing

19.____

20. Which of the following signifies the international reference model for linking different types of computers and networks?

    A. WAN   B. ISDN   C. TCP/IP   D. OSI

20.____

21. The main difference between neural networks and expert systems is that neural networks

    A. seek a generalized capability to learn
    B. program solutions
    C. are aimed at solving one specific problem at a time
    D. seek to emulate or model a person's way of solving a set of problems

21.____

22. Which of the following is not a management benefit associated with end-user development of information systems?

    A. Reduced application backlog
    B. Increased user satisfaction
    C. Simplified testing and documentation procedures
    D. Improved requirements determination

22.____

23. Which of the following is NOT an example of an output control associated with information systems?

    A. Balancing output totals with input and processing totals
    B. formal procedures and documentation specifying recipients of reports and checks
    C. Error handling
    D. Review of computer processing logs

23.____

24. Of the following statements about the evolutionary planning method of strategic informa-   24.__
    tion systems design, which is FALSE?
    It is

    A. a top-down method
    B. high adaptive
    C. best for use in a dynamic environment
    D. susceptible to domination by a few users

25. In a relational database, a row or record is referred to as a(n)   25.__

    A. applet   B. key field
    C. tuple   D. bitmap

_____

KEY (CORRECT ANSWERS)

1.	C	11.	D
2.	A	12.	B
3.	D	13.	B
4.	B	14.	D
5.	D	15.	D
6.	D	16.	B
7.	C	17.	B
8.	A	18.	B
9.	C	19.	C
10.	A	20.	D

21.	A
22.	C
23.	C
24.	A
25.	C

_____

TEST 2

DIRECTIONS: Each question or incomplete statement is followed by several suggested answers or completions. Select the one that BEST answers the question or completes the statement. *PRINT THE LETTER OF THE CORRECT ANSWER IN THE SPACE AT THE RIGHT.*

1. The technical staff of an organization are most likely to be users of a(n)   1._____

    A. transaction processing system (TPS)
    B. management information system (MIS)
    C. decision support system (DSS)
    D. knowledge work system (KWS)

2. The predefined packet of data in some LANs, which includes data indicating the sender,   2._____
receiver, and whether the packet is in use, is known as a

    A. bus   B. check   C. token   D. parity

3. Which of the following is NOT a typical characteristic of hypertext and hypermedia appli-   3._____
cations?

    A. Users given commands to delete frames
    B. Independence from GUI environment
    C. Frames displayed in windows
    D. In shared systems, concurrent access to hypermedia data

4. Which of the following is a commercial digital information service that exists to provide   4._____
business information?

    A. Prodigy   B. Dialog   C. Quotron   D. Lexis

5. Which of the following is NOT a characteristic of an enterprise MIS?   5._____

    A. Standardization
    B. Requires systems managers
    C. Homogeneous data
    D. Supports multiple applications

6. In workgroup information systems, the simplest type of group conferencing is referred to   6._____
as a(n)

    A. videoconference   B. group meeting
    C. asynchronous meeting   D. electronic bulletin board

7. Which of the following is an advantage associated with the LAN model of multi-user sys-   7._____
tems?

    A. Reliability of many computers
    B. Unlimited performance
    C. Centralized control
    D. Relative independence from technology

8. The main advantage of digital private branch exchanges over other local networking   8._____
options is that they

A. make use of existing phone lines
B. have a greater geographical range
C. perform important traffic control functions
D. can generally transmit larger volumes of data

9. In a typical organization, tactical and operational planning of an MIS would be the responsibility of the   9.__

    A. steering committee and MIS managers
    B. project teams
    C. operations personnel and end users
    D. chief information officer

10. _____ code is the term for program instructions written in a high-level language before translation into machine language.   10.__

    A. Spaghetti   B. Source   C. Macro   D. Pseudo

11. In its current form, the technology of electronic data interchange (EDI) is appropriate for transmitting all of the following EXCEPT   11.__

    A. purchase orders   B. bills of lading
    C. solicitations   D. invoices

12. Which of the following types of applications is generally most dependent on the graphical user interface (GUI) environment?   12.__

    A. Electronic communication
    B. Desktop publishing
    C. Word processing
    D. Spreadsheet

13. Which of the following is a logical design element of an information system?   13.__

    A. Hardware specifications   B. Output media
    C. Data models   D. Software

14. A processing system rejects an order transaction for 10,000 units, on the basis that no order larger than 70 units had been placed previously. This is an example of a   14.__

    A. check digit   B. format check
    C. reasonableness check   D. dependency check

15. The concentric circle on the surface area of a disk, on which data are stored as magnetized spots, is known as a   15.__

    A. cylinder   B. track   C. register   D. sector

16. Which of the following storage media generally has the slowest access speed?   16.__

    A. Optical disk   B. RAM
    C. Magnetic disk   D. Cache

17. The most time-consuming element of system conversion plans is   17.__

    A. hardware upgrading   B. personnel training
    C. documentation   D. data conversion

18. In most organizations, the chief information officer is given a rank equivalent to   18.____

    A. project manager
    B. data administrator
    C. team leader
    D. vice president

19. Which of the following statements about the prototyping approach to systems development is FALSE?   19.____
It is

    A. especially valuable for designing an end-user interface
    B. generally better suited for larger applications
    C. most useful when there is some uncertainty about requirements or design solutions
    D. as iterative process

20. What is the term for the final step in system reengineering, when the revised specifications are used to generate new, structure program code for a structured and maintainable system?   20.____

    A. Direct cutover
    B. Reverse engineering
    C. Workflow engineering
    D. Forward engineering

21. Which of the following are included in an MIS audit?   21.____
    I. Physical facilities
    II. Telecommunications
    III. Control systems
    IV. Manual procedures
The CORRECT answer is:

    A. I, IV
    B. II, III
    C. I, II, III
    D. I, II, III, IV

22. In the traditional systems life cycle model, which of the following stages occurs EARLIEST?   22.____

    A. Programming
    B. Design
    C. Installation
    D. Systems study

23. Which of the following concerns is addressed by front-end CASE (Computer-Assisted Software Engineering) tools?   23.____

    A. Testing
    B. Analysis
    C. Maintenance
    D. Coding

24. In an individual MIS, the most commonly used analytical application is a   24.____

    A. statistical program
    B. gateway
    C. spreadsheet
    D. utility

25. Certain kinds of expert systems use the property of inheritance to organize and classify knowledge when the knowledge base is composed of easily identifiable chunks or objects of interrelated characteristics. These systems are known specifically as   25.____

    A. political models
    B. rule bases
    C. formal control tools
    D. semantic nets

KEY (CORRECT ANSWERS)

1.	D		11.	C
2.	C		12.	B
3.	B		13.	C
4.	B		14.	C
5.	C		15.	B
6.	D		16.	C
7.	A		17.	D
8.	A		18.	D
9.	A		19.	B
10.	B		20.	D

21.	D
22.	D
23.	B
24.	C
25.	D

―――――――

TEST 3

DIRECTIONS: Each question or incomplete statement is followed by several suggested answers or completions. Select the one that BEST answers the question or completes the statement. *PRINT THE LETTER OF THE CORRECT ANSWER IN THE SPACE AT THE RIGHT.*

1. Of an organization's total MIS budget, the majority can be expected to be spent on   1.____

    A. training
    C. operations
    B. programming
    D. administration

2. Each of the following is an element of the installation stage in the traditional model of a systems life cycle EXCEPT   2.____

    A. testing
    C. conversion
    B. programming
    D. training

3. For network applications in which some processing must be centralized and some can be performed locally, which of the following configurations is most appropriate?   3.____

    A. Bus   B. Ring   C. Star   D. Token ring

4. In systems development, the main difference between strategic analysis and enterprise analysis is that   4.____

    A. enterprise analysis makes use of the personal interview
    B. enterprise analysis produces a smaller data set
    C. strategic analysis is used exclusively in profit concerns
    D. strategic analysis tends to have a broader focus

5. Each of the following is a type of source data automation technology EXCEPT   5.____

    A. magnetic ink character recognition (MICR)
    B. touch screen
    C. bar code
    D. optical character recognition (OCR)

6. The main DISADVANTAGE associated with the parallel strategy of information system conversion is that   6.____

    A. run and personnel costs are extremely high
    B. it presents many difficulties in the area of documentation
    C. it provides no fallback in case of trouble
    D. it does not provide a clear picture of how the system will eventually operate throughout the entire organization

7. Which of the following types of systems is most appropriate for solving unstructured problems?   7.____

    A. Expert system
    B. Executive support system (ESS)
    C. Management information system (MIS)
    D. Decision support system (DSS)

8. In terms of information ethics, what is the term for the existence of laws that permit individuals to recover damages done to them by actors, systems, or organizations?

    A. Liability   B. Subrogation
    C. Accountability   D. Due process

8.__

9. Descriptions that focus on the dynamic aspects of a system's structure, or on change, evolution, and processes in general, are described as

    A. charismatic   B. synchronic
    C. motile   D. diachronic

9.__

10. One of the features of object-oriented programming is that all objects in a certain group have all the characteristics of that group. This feature is defined as

    A. base   B. legitimacy
    C. class   D. multiplexing

10.__

11. The most prominent data manipulation language in use today is

    A. Intellect   B. Easytrieve
    C. APL   D. SQL

11.__

12. Feasibility studies involved in systems analysis tend to focus on three specific areas._____ feasibility is NOT one of these.

    A. Technical   B. Operational
    C. Cultural   D. Economic

12.__

13. A computer may sometimes handle programs more efficiently by dividing them into small fixed-or variable-length portions, with only a small portion stored in primary memory at one time. This is known as

    A. multitasking   B. caching
    C. allocation   D. virtual storage

13.__

14. Of the following applications, end-user computing is MOST appropriate for the development of

    A. scheduling systems for optimal production
    B. tracking daily trades of securities
    C. systems for handling air traffic
    D. systems for the development of three-dimensional graphics

14.__

15. In a hierarchical database, what is the term for the specialized data element attached to a record that shows the absolute or relative address of another record?

    A. Tickler   B. Index   C. Register   D. Pointer

15.__

16. For which of the following types of databases is the direct file access method most appropriate?

    A. Bank statements
    B. Payroll
    C. On-line hotel reservations
    D. Government benefits program

16.__

17. A _____ structured project with_____ technology requirements would most likely   17._____
involve the lowest degree of risk to an organization.

    A. small, highly; low   B. small, flexibly; high
    C. large, flexibly; high   D. large, highly; low

18. Historically, under federal law creators of intellectual property were protected against   18._____
copying by others for a period of

    A. 10 years
    B. 17 years
    C. 28 years
    D. the creator's natural life

19. Most modern secondary storage devices operate at speeds measured in   19._____

    A. nanoseconds   B. milliseconds
    C. microseconds   D. seconds

20. Which of the following signifies the international standard for transmitting voice, video,   20._____
and data to support a wide range of service over the public telephone lines?

    A. HTML   B. ISDN   C. TCP/IP   D. ASCII

21. An important limitation associated with executive support systems today is that they   21._____

    A. use data from different systems designed for very different purposes
    B. have a narrow range of easy-to-use desktop analytical tools
    C. are used almost exclusively by executives
    D. do an inadequate job of filtering data

22. Each of the following is an element of the systems study stage in the traditional model of   22._____
a systems life cycle EXCEPT

    A. identifying objectives to be attained by a solution
    B. determining whether the organization has a problem that can be solved with a system
    C. analyzing problems with existing systems
    D. describing alternative solutions

23. The commercial software product *Lotus Notes* is an example of   23._____

    A. intelligent agent software
    B. groupware
    C. a star network
    D. electronic data interchange (EDI)

24. Weaknesses in a system's _____ controls may create errors or failures in new or modi-   24._____
fied systems.

    A. data file security   B. implementation
    C. physical hardware   D. software

25. Which of the following is a term used to describe the ability to move from summary data to more specific levels of detail?   25.__

    A. Drill down
    C. Downsizing
                                        B. Forward chaining
                                        D. Semantic networking

---

KEY (CORRECT ANSWERS)

1.	C	11.	D
2.	B	12.	C
3.	C	13.	D
4.	D	14.	D
5.	B	15.	D
6.	A	16.	C
7.	B	17.	A
8.	A	18.	C
9.	D	19.	B
10.	C	20.	B

21.	A
22.	B
23.	B
24.	B
25.	A

EXAMINATION SECTION
TEST 1

DIRECTIONS: Each question or incomplete statement is followed by several suggested answers or completions. Select the one that BEST answers the question or completes the statement. *PRINT THE LETTER OF THE CORRECT ANSWER IN THE SPACE AT THE RIGHT.*

1. A microprocessor includes media for each of the following EXCEPT

    A. secondary storage   B. control
    C. logic   D. memory

1.____

2. Which of the following protocols is LEAST likely to be used in a wide-area network (WAN)?

    A. SNA   B. Token passing
    C. TCP/IP   D. DEC DNA

2.____

3. In an expert system, the rule base is sometimes searched using a strategy that begins with a hypothesis and seeks out more information until the hypothesis is either proved or disproved. This strategy is known as

    A. backward chaining
    B. key fielding
    C. indexed sequential access
    D. process specification

3.____

4. The meaning of signs, symbols, messages or systems are involved in a body of inquiry known as

    A. linguistics   B. semantics
    C. communications   D. syntactics

4.____

5. Which of the following is a query language?

    A. Nomad   B. Ideal   C. Systat   D. RPG-III

5.____

6. Which of the following is the typical unit of measurement used by systems designers to estimate the length of time needed to complete a project?

    A. Data-week   B. Man-hour
    C. File-hour   D. Man-month

6.____

7. Which of the following is the oldest professional computer society in the United States?

    A. Data Processing Management Association (DPMA)
    B. Institute for Certification of Computer Professionals (ICP)
    C. Association of Computing Machinery (ACM)
    D. Information Technology Association of America (ITAA)

7.____

8. Which of the following terms is commonly used to describe the interaction of people and machines in the work environment, especially in terms of job design and health issues?

    A. Connectivity   B. Ergonomics
    C. Feasibility   D. Interface

8.____

9. Which of the following is a likely application of the sensitivity analysis models of a decision–support system?   9.__

    A. Forecasting sales
    B. Determining the proper product mix within a given market
    C. Predicting the actions of competitors
    D. Goal seeking

10. What is the term for the temporary storage location in a control unit where small amounts of data or instructions reside for thousandths of a second just before use?   10.__

    A. Cache   B. Register   C. Sector   D. Buffer

11. Systems whose behavior includes options without specification of probabilities within the system are described as   11.__

    A. runaway   B. possibilistic
    C. stochastic   D. probabilistic

12. The physical devices and software that link various hardware components and transfer data from one physical location to another are known collectively as   12.__

    A. cyberspace
    B. wide–area networks
    C. telecommunications technology
    D. semantic networks

13. Which of the following is a tangible benefit associated with organizational information systems?   13.__

    A. Streamlined operations   B. Higher asset utilization
    C. Inventory reduction   D. Improved planning

14. Which of the following is NOT generally considered to be a physical component of an MIS?   14.__

    A. Personnel   B. Information
    C. Procedures   D. Software

15. Any undesired information in a communication channel which is not part of the intended message is typically referred to as   15.__

    A. resistance   B. noise
    C. data error   D. cross–talk

16. Which of the following is the ASCII 8–bit binary code for the number 1?   16.__

    A. 0001 0001   B. 0101 0001
    C. 0000 1000   D. 1001 0001

17. Which of the following is a method of organizing expert system knowledge into chunks in which relationships are based on shared characteristics determined by the user?   17.__

    A. Indexing   B. GUI
    C. Batch processing   D. Frames

18. Which of the following is a telecommunications requirement that is particular to the task   18.____
of on–line data entry?

    A.   High–capacity video and data capabilities
    B.   Infrequent, high–volume bursts of information
    C.   Instant response
    D.   Direct response

19. What is the term for the technology which breaks blocks of text into small fixed bundles of   19.____
data and routes them in an economical way through an available communications channel?

    A.   Optical character recognition
    B.   Frame relay
    C.   Packet switching
    D.   Branch exchange

20. A transaction processing system rejects a transaction on the basis that it includes a   20.____
Social Security number which contains an alphabetic character. This is an example of
a(n) _____ check.

    A.   reasonableness   B.   format
    C.   dependency   D.   existence

21. The smallest unit of data for defining an image in a computer is the   21.____

    A. byte   B. pixel   C. quark   D. bit

22. In a microcomputer, which of the following transmits signals specifying whether to read or   22.____
write data from a given primary storage address, input device, or output device?

    A.   Control bus   B.   Address bus
    C.   Data bus   D.   CPU

23. Which of the following stages occurs the LATEST in the traditional systems life cycle   23.____
model?

    A.   Systems study   B.   Programming
    C.   Design   D.   Project definition

24. The fastest and most expensive memory used in a microcomputer is located in the   24.____

    A. cache   B. register   C. hard disk   D. RAM

25. Which of the following is an optical disk system that allows users to record data only   25.____
once, but to read the data indefinitely?

    A. WORM   B. EPROM   C. RAM   D. TQM

KEY (CORRECT ANSWERS)

1.	A		11.	B
2.	B		12.	C
3.	A		13.	C
4.	B		14.	B
5.	D		15.	B
6.	D		16.	B
7.	C		17.	D
8.	B		18.	D
9.	D		19.	C
10.	B		20.	B

21.	B
22.	A
23.	B
24.	B
25.	A

TEST 2

DIRECTIONS: Each question or incomplete statement is followed by several suggested answers or completions. Select the one that BEST answers the question or completes the statement. *PRINT THE LETTER OF THE CORRECT ANSWER IN THE SPACE AT THE RIGHT.*

1. Which of the following styles of systems development is most often used for information systems at the individual level?

    A. End–user computing
    B. Commercial software packages
    C. Prototyping
    D. Traditional life cycle

1.____

2. Which of the following is a programming language that was developed in 1956 for scientific and mathematical applications?

    A. COBOL   B. BASIC   C. Pascal   D. FORTRAN

2.____

3. Which of the following personnel would be considered a *technical specialist* in an MIS department?

    A. Education specialist   B. Database administrator
    C. Applications programmer   D. Systems analyst

3.____

4. Which of the following is NOT a characteristic of a fault–tolerant system?

    A. The use of special software routines to detect hardware failures
    B. Extra memory chips, processors, and disk storage
    C. Continuous detection of bugs or program defects
    D. Hardware parts that can be removed without system disruption

4.____

5. Defining a system program in such a way that it may call itself is an example of

    A. eudemony   B. recursion
    C. redundancy   D. artificial intelligence

5.____

6. What is the term used to enumerate the number of bits that can be processed at one time by a computer?

    A. Data bus width   B. Word length
    C. RAM capacity   D. Bandwidth

6.____

7. Which of the following is another term for a field, or a grouping of characters into a word, group of words, or complete number?

    A. Code   B. Byte
    C. Data element   D. File

7.____

8. A person in a multi–user system sends a message using the OSI model to another user at a different location. At the messenger's end of the system, after passing through the *session* layer of the model, the message will then enter the _____ layer.

    A. transport   B. network
    C. presentation   D. data link

8.____

9. Which of the following is NOT a disadvantage associated with the traditional life cycle model of systems development?

   A. Time consumption
   B. Oversimplification
   C. Cost
   D. Inflexibility

9.__

10. Transmission speeds that would fall within the expected range of coaxial cable are _____ per second.

    A. 400 bits
    B. 50 megabits
    C. 300 megabits
    D. 7 gigabits

10.__

11. Which of the following is a telecommunications computer that collects and temporarily stores messages from terminals for batch transmission to the host computer?

    A. Assembler
    B. Concentrator
    C. Buffer
    D. Compiler

11.__

12. Which of the following is an advantage associated with the centralized or teleprocessing model of multi–user systems?

    A. Local computing
    B. Scaleability
    C. Low start–up costs
    D. Low technical risk

12.__

13. Software systems that can operate on different hardware platforms are referred to as _____ systems.

    A. open
    B. interoperable
    C. branched
    D. transmigrational

13.__

14. What is the term for the process by which the properties of a collection (i.e., of data) are described in terms of the sums of the properties of the units contained in the collection?

    A. Unity
    B. Autarky
    C. Chunking
    D. Aggregation

14.__

15. In systems terminology, what is the term for output that is returned to the appropriate members of an organization to help them evaluate or correct input?

    A. Exit data
    B. Feedback
    C. Assessor
    D. Valuation

15.__

16. The years 1957 to 1963 are generally considered to have been the _____ generation in the evolution of computer hardware technology.

    A. first
    B. second
    C. third
    D. fourth

16.__

17. A conversion approach in which the new system completely replaces the old one on an appointed day is known as

    A. focused differentiation
    B. direct cutover
    C. allied distribution
    D. batch processing

17.__

18. Of the following types of business network redesign, the one that can be said to be most highly coupled is/are   18.____

    A. interenterprise system access
    B. knowledge networks
    C. EDI
    D. interenterprise process integration

19. Which of the following terms is used to describe the shape or configuration of a telecommunications network?   19.____

    A. Duplex   B. Topology
    C. Protocol   D. Transmissivity

20. Which of the following is/are recognized differences between microcomputers and workstations?   20.____

    I. Microcomputers have more powerful mathematical processing capabilities.
    II. Microcomputers are more useful for computer–aided design (CAD).
    III. Workstations are more widely used by knowledge workers.
    IV. Workstations can more easily perform multiple tasks simultaneously.
The CORRECT answer is:

    A. I, II   B. II, III   C. III, IV   D. II, IV

21. Which of the following signifies a tool for retrieving and transferring files from a remote computer?   21.____

    A. EDI   B. CPU   C. TCP/IP   D. FTP

22. Which of the following is a federal privacy law that applies to private institutions?   22.____

    A. Freedom of Information Act of 1968 (as amended)
    B. Privacy Act of 1974 (as amended)
    C. Privacy Protection Act of 1980
    D. Computer Matching and Privacy Protection Act of 1988

23. The main contribution of end–user systems development typically occurs in the area of   23.____

    A. productivity enhancement
    B. improved updating functions
    C. increased technical complexity
    D. improved efficiency in transaction processing

24. In cooperative processing, a mainframe and a microcomputer generally share tasks. The mainframe, however, is generally best at performing   24.____

    A. screen presentation   B. error processing
    C. data field editing   D. file input and output

25. In a systems development process, users are made active members of development   25.___
    project teams, and some users are placed in charge of system training and installation.
    In this case, management has made use of _____ tools.

    A. external integration   B. internal integration
    C. formal planning   D. formal control

_____

KEY (CORRECT ANSWERS)

1.	C		11.	B
2.	D		12.	D
3.	B		13.	A
4.	C		14.	D
5.	B		15.	B
6.	B		16.	B
7.	C		17.	B
8.	A		18.	B
9.	B		19.	B
10.	B		20.	C

21.	D
22.	C
23.	A
24.	D
25.	A

_____

TEST 3

DIRECTIONS: Each question or incomplete statement is followed by several suggested answers or completions. Select the one that BEST answers the question or completes the statement. *PRINT THE LETTER OF THE CORRECT ANSWER IN THE SPACE AT THE RIGHT.*

1. As a general rule, the development of a system that will be used by others can be expected to take_____ as long as the development of an individual system that will be used only by the developer.

    A.   half   B.   twice
    C.   three times   D.   five times

1.____

2. In LANs, the token ring configuration is most useful for

    A.   broadcasting messages to the entire network through a single circuit
    B.   multidirectional transmissions between microcomputers or between micros and a larger computer
    C.   transmissions between microcomputers and a larger computer that require a degree of traffic control
    D.   transmitting large volumes of data between microcomputers

2.____

3. Which of the following statements about expert systems is generally TRUE? They

    A.   function best in lower–level clerical functions
    B.   require minimal development resources
    C.   are highly adaptable over time
    D.   are capable of representing a wide range of causal models

3.____

4. A middle–range machine with a RAM capacity that measures from about 10 megabytes to over 1 gigabyte is known as a

    A.   microcomputer   B.   minicomputer
    C.   desktop computer   D.   mainframe

4.____

5. Which of the following media uses the sector method for storing data?

    A.   Cache   B.   Floppy disk
    C.   Hard disk   D.   CD–ROM

5.____

6. When mechanisms of functional subsystems are connected causally to influence each other, they are said to be

    A.   aggregated   B.   coupled
    C.   synchronous   D.   constrained

6.____

7. Which of the following storage media generally has the largest capacity?

    A.   Cache   B.   Magnetic disk
    C.   Optical disk   D.   Magnetic tape

7.____

8. In terms of information ethics, the mechanisms for assessing responsibility for decisions and actions are referred to as

    A.   liability   B.   capacity
    C.   creditability   D.   accountability

8.____

9. Which of the following signifies the central switching system that handles a firm's voice and digital communications?

    A. OSI   B. DSS   C. PBX   D. LAN

9.__

10. What is the term for the LAN channel technology that provides a single path for transmitting text, graphics, voice, or video data at one time?

    A. Bus   B. Baseband
    C. Firewall   D. Broadband

10.__

11. The stage in a system's life cycle in which testing, training, and conversion occur is termed

    A. evaluation   B. design
    C. installation   D. documentation

11.__

12. Which of the following is NOT a type of processor used in telecommunications systems?

    A. Coaxial cable   B. Controller
    C. Modem   D. Multiplexer

12.__

13. A database that is stored in more than one physical location is described as

    A. sequential   B. wide-area
    C. distributed   D. indexed

13.__

14. An organization decides to redesign its information system using only the components that are already available to it. In the language of systems theory, the resulting system would be described as a(n)

    A. ensemble   B. creod   C. kluge   D. cyborg

14.__

15. What is the term for an integrated circuit made by printing thousands or millions of transistors on a small silicon chip?

    A. Cache   B. Semiconductor
    C. Control unit   D. Microprocessor

15.__

16. Computer programming includes a logic pattern that allows for the repetition of certain actions while a specified condition occurs or until a certain conditions exists. This pattern is known as the

    A. object linkage   B. selection construct
    C. key field   D. iteration construct

16.__

17. Which of the following is the standard or reference model for allowing e-mail systems operating on different hardware to communicate?

    A. X.400   B. X.25   C. X.12   D. FDDI

17.__

18. Which of the following terms is used to denote circular tracks on the same vertical line within a disk pack?

    A. Track   B. Spindle   C. Sector   D. Cylinder

18.__

19. A system that is capable of listing the descriptions of each of a certain set of alternatives   19.____
is described as

    A. generative   B. contingency–based
    C. smart   D. stochastic

20. Which of the following is an operating cost associated with an information system?   20.____

    A. Database establishment   B. Facilities
    C. Personnel training   D. Hardware acquisition

21. As a collaboration tool, the World Wide Web involves   21.____

    A. data that undergoes frequent updating
    B. documents predominantly authored by a single user
    C. applications with data at multiple sites
    D. applications with high security requirements

22. A mathematical formula used to translate a record's key field directly into its storage loca-   22.____
tion is known as a(n) _____ algorithm.

    A. synchronous   B. genetic
    C. asynchronous   D. transform

23. Which of the following is a common DISADVANTAGE associated with outsourcing the   23.____
systems development process?

    A. Loss of control over system function
    B. Increased costs
    C. Generally slow progress
    D. Increased paperwork requirements

24. Which of the following is a network topology in which all computers and other devices are   24.____
connected to a central host computer?

    A. LAN   B. Star   C. Ring   D. Bus

25. In terms of information systems, *processing* means the   25.____

    A. assignment of data to certain categories for later use
    B. calculation or computation of data to arrive at a solution or conclusion
    C. conversion, manipulation, and analysis of raw input into a meaningful form
    D. collection or capture of raw data for use in an information system

———————

KEY (CORRECT ANSWERS)

1.	C	11.	C
2.	D	12.	A
3.	A	13.	C
4.	B	14.	C
5.	B	15.	B
6.	B	16.	D
7.	C	17.	A
8.	D	18.	D
9.	C	19.	A
10.	B	20.	B

21.	B
22.	D
23.	A
24.	B
25.	C

EXAMINATION SECTION
TEST 1

DIRECTIONS: Each question or incomplete statement is followed by several suggested answers or completions. Select the one that BEST answers the question or completes the statement. *PRINT THE LETTER OF THE CORRECT ANSWER IN THE SPACE AT THE RIGHT.*

1. What is the term for a device that enables a single communications channel to carry data transmissions from many different sources simultaneously?   1.____

    A. Compiler   B. Multitasker
    C. Concentrator   D. Multiplexer

2. Which of the following represents the earliest stage in the computer language translation process?   2.____

    A. Linkage editor   B. Load module
    C. Compiler   D. Object code

3. Within data flow diagrams, the transformations that occur within the lowest level are described by   3.____

    A. development methodologies
    B. structure charts
    C. selection constructs
    D. process specifications

4. The time or number of operations after which a process in a system repeats itself is expressed in a measure known as   4.____

    A. periodicity   B. synchronicity
    C. loop   D. iteration

5. What is the term for the single steps or actions in the logic of a program that do NOT depend on the existence of any condition?   5.____

    A. Logical construct   B. Run control
    C. Sequence construct   D. Rule base

6. Which of the following terms is most different in meaning from the others?   6.____

    A. Data file approach
    B. Relational data model
    C. Flat file organization
    D. Traditional file environment

7. Which of the following is a tool for locating data on the Internet that performs key word searches of an actual database of documents, software, and data files available for downloading?   7.____

    A. WAIS   B. Archie   C. Acrobat   D. Gopher

8. Typical transaction processing (TPS) systems include all of the following types EXCEPT _____ systems.   8.____

    A. finance/accounting   B. sales/marketing
    C. engineering/design   D. human resources

9. The main weakness of the enterprise analysis approach to systems development is that it   9.__

    A. involves little input at the managerial level
    B. is relatively unstructured
    C. produces an enormous amount of data that is expensive to collect and analyze
    D. only generally identifies an organization's informational requirements

10. What is the term for special system software that translates a higher–level language into machine language for execution by the computer?   10.__

    A. Compiler   B. Translator   C. Renderer   D. Assembler

11. Compared to private branch exchanges, LANs   11.__
    I. are more expensive to install
    II. have a smaller geographical range
    III. are more inflexible
    IV. require specially trained staff
The CORRECT answer is

    A. I only   B. I, III
    C. I, II, IV   D. III, IV

12. Each of the following is considered to be a basic component of a database management system EXCEPT a   12.__

    A. transform algorithm
    B. data manipulation language
    C. data definition language
    D. data dictionary

13. Which of the following is a technical approach to the study of information systems?   13.__

    A. Management science   B. Sociology
    C. Political science   D. Psychology

14. In desktop publishing applications, a user may sometimes elect to alter the standard spacing between two characters. This is a technique known as   14.__

    A. weighting   B. kerning   C. pointing   D. leading

15. In systems design, the generic framework used to think '. about a problem is known as the   15.__

    A. schema   B. reference model
    C. prototype   D. operational model

16. What is the term for a small computer that manages! communications for the host computer in a network?   16.__

    A. Concentrator   B. Multiplexer
    C. Controller   D. Front–end processor

17. Which of the following is a competitive strategy for developing new market niches, where   17.____
a business can compete in a target area better than its competitors?

   A. Vertical integration   B. Focused differentiation
   C. Multitasking   D. Forward engineering

18. An electronic meeting system (EMS) is considered to be a type of collaborative   18.____

   A. executive support system (ESS)
   B. management information system (MIS)
   C. office automation system (OAS)
   D. group decision support system (GDSS)

19. In systems theory, the minimum description required to distinguish a system from its   19.____
environment is known as a(n)

   A. blip   B. margin   C. mediation   D. boundary

20. The principal advantage of the hierarchical and network database models is   20.____

   A. adaptability
   B. architecture simplicity
   C. minimal programming requirements
   D. processing efficiency

21. Which of the following is a character–oriented tool for locating data on the Internet which   21.____
allows a user to locate textual information through a series of hierarchical menus?

   A. FTP   B. Gopher   C. Lug   D. Archie

22. The principal logical database models include each of the following types EXCEPT   22.____

   A. network   B. object–oriented
   C. relational   D. hierarchical

23. Computer programming includes a logic pattern where a stated condition determines   23.____
which of two or more actions can be taken, depending on the condition. This pattern is
known as the

   A. object linkage   B. selection construct
   C. key field   D. iteration construct

24. Which of the following is the tool used by database designers to document a conceptual   24.____
data model?

   A. Entity–relationship diagram
   B. Partition statement
   C. Gantt chart
   D. Data–flow diagram

25. The phenomenon of _____ refers to the idea that people will avoid new uncertain alternatives and stick with traditional and familiar rules and procedures. 25.__

    A. the Hawthorne effect
    B. bounded rationality
    C. system–oriented reasoning
    D. case–based reasoning

_____

KEY (CORRECT ANSWERS)

1.	D	11.	C
2.	C	12.	A
3.	D	13.	A
4.	A	14.	B
5.	C	15.	B
6.	B	16.	D
7.	B	17.	B
8.	C	18.	D
9.	C	19.	D
10.	A	20.	D

21.	B
22.	B
23.	B
24.	A
25.	B

_____

TEST 2

DIRECTIONS: Each question or incomplete statement is followed by several suggested answers or completions. Select the one that BEST answers the question or completes the statement. *PRINT THE LETTER OF THE CORRECT ANSWER IN THE SPACE AT THE RIGHT.*

1. In systems theory, the history of a system's structural transformations is referred to as its   1.____

   A. ontology
   C. ontogeny

   B. entailment
   D. epistemology

2. Programming language that consists of the 1s and 0s of binary code is referred to as   2.____

   A. machine language
   C. object language

   B. assemblage
   D. pseudocode

3. Generally, the EBCDIC standard can be used to code up to _____ characters in one byte of information.   3.____

   A. 128   B. 256   C. 512   D. 1024

4. In MIS terminology, which of the following offers the best definition of *network?*   4.____

   A. The devices and software that link components and transfer data from one location to another
   B. The media and software governing the storage and organization of data for use
   C. Two or more computers linked to share data or resources such as a printer
   D. Formal rules for accomplishing tasks

5. Which of the following is a type of MIS application used for analysis?   5.____

   A. Database
   C. Desktop publishing

   B. Operations research
   D. Presentation

6. In computer processing, an overload sometimes results when trying to test more rules to reach a solution that the computer is capable of handling. This type of overload is referred to as   6.____

   A. combinatorial explosion
   C. transaction jam

   B. data crashing
   D. conversion error

7. In the normal processing of a workgroup information system, which of the following is an operations procedure, as opposed to a user procedure?   7.____

   A. Maintaining backup
   B. Placing constraints on processing
   C. Initiating access to network
   D. Starting hardware and programs

8. A company's European units want to share information about production schedules and inventory levels to ship excess products from one country to another. The telecommunications technology most appropriate for this is   8.____

   A. teleconferencing
   C. e-mail

   B. voice mail
   D. videoconferencing

9. As opposed to systems development, approximately how much of an organization's   9.___
   efforts can be expected to be spent on systems maintenance during the total system life
   cycle?

   A. 25   B. 45   C. 65   D. 85

10. The most critical, and often most difficult, task of the systems analyst is usually to   10.___

   A. define the specific problem that must be solved with an information system
   B. identify the causes of the problem
   C. specify the nature of the solution that will address the problem
   D. define the specific information requirements that must be met by the system solu-
       tion

11. Which of the following is not a commonly recognized difference between workgroup and   11.___
    enterprise management information systems?

   A. An enterprise MIS is a subfunction of a company.
   B. Workgroup MIS users know and work with each other,
   C. An enterprise MIS uses several different applications.
   D. A workgroup MIS is a peripheral system.

12. The first step in testing the accuracy of a spreadsheet application is usually to   12.___

   A. verify the input
   B. stresstest the spreadsheet
   C. check the output
   D. involve others in the process

13. Programs in information systems make use of complete, unambiguous procedures for   13.___
    solving specified problems in a finite number of steps. These procedures are known as

   A. schema   B. protocols
   C. algorithms   D. criteria

14. Weaknesses in a system's_____ controls may permit unauthorized changes in pro-   14.___
    cessing.

   A. software   B. computer operations
   C. data file security   D. implementation

15. In the model of case–based reasoning, after a user describes a problem, the system   15.___

   A. modifies its solution to better fit the problem
   B. asks the user questions to narrow its search
   C. retrieves a solution
   D. searches a database for a similar problem

16. The particular form that information technology takes in a specific organization to achieve   16.___
    selected goals or functions is referred to as the organization's

   A. information configuration
   B. knowledge base
   C. operability
   D. information architecture

17. Which of the following applications is most likely to require real–time response from a telecommunications network?

    A. Intercomputer data exchange
    B. Administrative message switching
    C. Process control
    D. On–line text retrieval

17.____

18. The main DISADVANTAGE associated with the use of application software packages to solve organizational problems is that

    A. the initial costs of purchase are often prohibitive
    B. they often involve the added costs of customization and additional programming
    C. maintenance and support will usually have to come from within the purchasing organization
    D. the new program usually requires intensive training

18.____

19. Which of the following is a disadvantage associated with distributed data processing?

    A. Drains on system power
    B. Reliance on high–end telecommunications technology
    C. Increased vulnerability of storage location
    D. Reduced responsiveness to local users

19.____

20. In the current environment of systems development, end–user computing contributes most effectively to the _____ aspects of the process.

    A. problem identification and systems study
    B. installation and maintenance
    C. systems study and installation
    D. programming and detail design

20.____

21. Which of the following steps in the machine cycle of a computer occurs during the execution cycle (e–cycle)?

    A. Instruction fetched
    B. Data sent from main memory to storage register
    C. Instruction decoded
    D. Instruction placed into instruction register

21.____

22. Of the following, which offers the least accurate definition of *information* as it applies to the study of MIS?

    A. Data placed within a context
    B. The amount of uncertainty that is reduced when a message is received
    C. A thing or things that are known to have occurred, to exist, or to be true
    D. Knowledge derived from data

22.____

23. Programming languages in which each source code statement generates multiple statements at the machine–language level are described as

    A. incremental   B. high–level
    C. first–generation   D. hierarchical

23.____

24. Which of the following types of visual representations is used as an overview, to depict   24.__
an entire system as a single process with its major inputs and outputs?

    A.   Context diagram   B.   Decision tree
    C.   Data flow diagram   D.   Nomograph

25. Once an organization has developed a business telecommunications plan, it must deter-   25.__
mine the initial scope of the project, taking several factors into account. The first and
most important of these factors is

    A.   security   B.   connectivity
    C.   distance   D.   multiple access

KEY (CORRECT ANSWERS)

1.	C		11.	A
2.	A		12.	C
3.	B		13.	C
4.	C		14.	A
5.	B		15.	D
6.	A		16.	D
7.	D		17.	D
8.	C		18.	B
9.	C		19.	B
10.	D		20.	D

21.	B
22.	C
23.	B
24.	A
25.	C

TEST 3

DIRECTIONS: Each question or incomplete statement is followed by several suggested answers or completions. Select the one that BEST answers the question or completes the statement. *PRINT THE LETTER OF THE CORRECT ANSWER IN THE SPACE AT THE RIGHT.*

1. Which of the following is a commonly used term for the programming environment of an expert system?

    A. Model   B. Ada   C. Schema   D. AI shell

1.____

2. In the language of dataflow diagrams, the external entity that absorbs a dataflow is known as a

    A. store   B. sink   C. cache   D. source

2.____

3. Which of the following is most clearly a fault tolerant technology?

    A. Random access memory
    B. On–line transaction processing
    C. Secondary storage
    D. Mobile data networks

3.____

4. Each of the following is a type of input control used with applications EXCEPT

    A. data conversion   B. run control totals
    C. edit checks   D. batch control totals

4.____

5. In a typical organization, approximately what percentage of total system maintenance time is spent making user enhancements, improving documentation, and recoding system components?

    A. 20   B. 40   C. 60   D. 80

5.____

6. Which of the following is NOT considered to be an operations control used with information systems?

    A. Error detection circuitry
    B. Control of equipment maintenance
    C. Regulated access to data centers
    D. Control of archival storage

6.____

7. Which of the following styles of systems development is most often used for information systems at the workgroup level?

    A. Traditional life cycle
    B. Life cycle for licensed programs
    C. Prototyping
    D. Outsourcing

7.____

8. Which of the following systems exists at the management level of an organization?

    A. Decision support system (DSS)
    B. Executive support system (ESS)
    C. Office automation system (OAS)
    D. Expert system

8.____

9. What is the term for a special language translator that translates each source code statement into machine code and executes it one at a time?

    A. Adapter   B. Assembler
    C. Compiler   D. Interpreter

9.___

10. Which of the following is NOT perceived to be a difference between a decision support system and a management information system?

    A. In an MIS, systems analysis is aimed at identifying information requirements.
    B. The philosophy of a DSS is to provide integrated tools, data, and models to users.
    C. The design process of an MIS is never really considered to be finished.
    D. The design of a DSS is an interative process.

10.___

11. Which of the following is a programming language that resembles machine language but substitutes mnemonics for numeric codes?

    A. Pseudocode   B. BASIC
    C. C   D. Assembly language

11.___

12. Each of the following is a rule of thumb for handling type in desktop publishing applications EXCEPT

    A. use small capitals for acronyms
    B. use sans serif typefaces when presenting a lot of text
    C. generally limit the different number of typefaces in a document to two
    D. use distinctly different typefaces together in the same document

12.___

13. Typically, a microcomputer is classified as a desktop or portable machine that has up to

    A. 1 gigabyte of secondary storage space
    B. 5 gigabytes of secondary storage space
    C. 64 megabytes of RAM
    D. 1 gigabyte of RAM

13.___

14. Which of the following is NOT considered to be a basic component of a decision support system?

    A. Electronic meeting system
    B. Database
    C. DSS software system
    D. Model base

14.___

15. Information systems that monitor the elementary activities and transactions of the organization are said to be functioning at the_____ level.

    A. tactical   B. operational
    C. strategic   D. managerial

15.___

16. Which of the following applications would be most likely to use the sequential method of file organization in a database?　　16.____

    A. Personnel evaluations
    B. Inventory
    C. Asset turnover calculations
    D. Payroll

17. Each of the following is a reason for the increased vulnerability of computerized systems to external threats EXCEPT　　17.____

    A. invisible appearance of procedures
    B. inability to replicate manually
    C. wider overall impact than manual systems
    D. multiple points of access

18. Membership functions are nonspecific terms that are used to solve problems in applications of　　18.____

    A. decision support   B. expert systems
    C. neural networks   D. fuzzy logic

19. Rules or standards used to rank alternatives in order of desirability are known as　　19.____

    A. norms   B. algorithms
    C. parameters   D. criteria

20. In most organizations, the database administration group performs each of the following functions EXCEPT　　20.____

    A. developing security procedures
    B. performing data quality audits
    C. maintaining database management software
    D. defining and organizing database structure and content

21. What is the term for on–line data that appears in the form of fixed–format reports for management executives?　　21.____

    A. Browsers   B. Briefing books
    C. Modules   D. Web pages

22. Which of the following is a likely application of the optimization models of a decision–support system?　　22.____

    A. Forecasting sales
    B. Determining the proper product mix within a given market
    C. Predicting the actions of competitors
    D. Goal seeking

23. In database management, a group of related fields is known as a(n)　　23.____

    A. domain   B. register   C. record   D. file

24. Storage of _____ is NOT a function of a computer's primary. storage.   24.__

    A. operating system programs
    B. data being used by the program
    C. all or part of the program being executed
    D. long–term data in a nonvolatile space

25. Which of the following is equal to 1 billion bytes of information?   25.__

    A. Nanobyte   B. Gigabyte   C. Terabyte   D. Megabyte

KEY (CORRECT ANSWERS)

1.	D		11.	D
2.	B		12.	B
3.	B		13.	C
4.	B		14.	A
5.	C		15.	B
6.	A		16.	D
7.	B		17.	C
8.	A		18.	D
9.	D		19.	D
10.	C		20.	B

21.	B
22.	B
23.	C
24.	D
25.	B

EXAMINATION SECTION
TEST 1

DIRECTIONS: Each question or incomplete statement is followed by several suggested answers or completions. Select the one that BEST answers the question or completes the statement. *PRINT THE LETTER OF THE CORRECT ANSWER IN THE SPACE AT THE RIGHT.*

1. What is the term for the methodical simplification of a logical data model? 1.____

    A. Elucidation   B. Normalization
    C. Partitioning   D. Bit streaming

2. Systems development projects _____ are most likely to benefit from the use of internal integration tools. 2.____

    A. with high levels of technical complexity
    B. in which end-user participation is voluntary
    C. which experience counterimplementation
    D. that are small in scale and involve only specific departments

3. In a typical telecommunications system, a message that has just passed through the front-end multiplexer will then pass through 3.____

    A. a front-end processor   B. a modem or modems
    C. a controller   D. the host computer

4. Which of the following is a characteristic of data warehouse data? They 4.____

    A. are organized from a functional view
    B. are volatile to support operations within a company
    C. include enterprise-wide data, collected from legacy systems
    D. involve individual fields that may be inconsistent across the enterprise

5. Which of the following terms is used to enumerate the bits that can be moved at one time between a CPU, primary storage, and other devices of a computer? 5.____

    A. Bandwidth   B. RAM cache
    C. Data bus width   D. Register

6. In enterprise analysis, data elements are organized into groups that support related sets of organizational processes. These groups are known as 6.____

    A. data sub-units   B. critical success factors
    C. end-user interfaces   D. logical application groups

7. Which of the following terms is used to describe a system's order of complexity? 7.____

    A. Resilience   B. Eudemony
    C. Ordinality   D. Dialectics

8. Of the following file organization methods, the only one that can be used on magnetic tape is 8.____

    A. random   B. indexed sequential
    C. alphabetic   D. sequential

9. What is the term for a set of rules and procedures that govern transmissions between the components of a telecommunications network?   9.__

    A. Criteria   B. Norms
    C. Algorithms   D. Protocols

10. In what type of processing can more than one instruction be processed at once, by breaking down a problem into smaller parts and processing them simultaneously?   10.__

    A. Parallel   B. Indexed
    C. Sequential   D. Batch

11. Which of the following terms is used to describe a system in which the internal parameters can be changed when necessary through feedback?   11.__

    A. Homeostatic   B. Elastic
    C. Capacitive   D. Heuristic

12. Each of the following is a rule of thumb for handling graphics in desktop publishing applications EXCEPT   12.__

    A. using pie charts for showing parts of a whole
    B. showing data relationships with line plots
    C. using serif typefaces in graph labels
    D. using bar charts to shown quantities of a single item

13. The central liability-related ethical issue raised by new information technologies is generally considered to be   13.__

    A. whether software or other intellectual property may be copied for personal use
    B. the point at which it is justifiable to release software or services for consumption by others
    C. the conditions under which it is justifiable to invade the privacy of others
    D. whether individuals and organizations that create, produce, and sell systems are morally responsible for the consequences of their use

14. Which of the following personnel would be considered part of the development team in an MIS department?   14.__

    A. Control clerk   B. Maintenance programmer
    C. Education specialist   D. Data administrator

15. Which of the following is an object-oriented programming language that can deliver only the software functionality needed for a particular task, and which can run on any computer or operating system?   15.__

    A. Perl   B. C   C. Linux   D. Java

16. Which of the following is NOT typically an example of the inquiry/response type of telecommunications application?   16.__

    A. Point-of-sale system
    B. Airline reservation system
    C. Hospital information system
    D. Credit checking

17. Which of the following is an example of work-flow management?   17.____

    A. Financial officers at a firm use a computer program to calculate the rate of return for specific investments.

    B. A manager views a company's quarterly revenues from her own workstation without the need for printed matter.

    C. Loan officers at a bank enter application information into a central system so that the application can be evaluated by many people at once.

    D. Cashiers at a retail outlet scan the bar codes on items of merchandise to more quickly move customers through the checkout.

18. According to Simon's description, there are four stages in any decision-making process. Decision support systems are designed primarily to help monitor the _____ stage.   18.____

    A. implementation   B. design
    C. choice   D. intelligence

19. A form of organization resembling a fishnet or network, in which authority is determined by knowledge and function, is a   19.____

    A. hierarchy   B. matrix
    C. heterarchy   D. homeostat

20. What is the term used to describe the approach to software development that combines data and procedures into a single item?   20.____

    A. Operational   B. Object-oriented
    C. Output controlled   D. Transactional

21. Which of the following is a computer language that is an application generator?   21.____

    A. SQL   B. Nomad   C. AMAPS   D. FOCUS

22. Approximately what percentage of an organization's software development budget will be expended on testing?   22.____

    A. 10-20   B. 15-35   C. 30-50   D. 55-75

23. The process embodied in an input-output device, which enables it to convert or code without memory a type of signal, motion, or sequence of characters into another, is known as   23.____

    A. telematics   B. polarity
    C. reification   D. transduction

24. Which of the following steps in the business systems planning (BSP) process is typically performed FIRST?   24.____

    A. Defining business processes

    B. Analyzing current systems support

    C. Defining information architecture

    D. Developing recommendations

25. What is the term for a networking technology that parcels information into 8-byte cells, allowing data to be transmitted between computers of different vendors at any speed?   25._

    A. Indexed sequential access method (ISAM)
    B. Asynchronous transfer mode (ATM)
    C. Private branch exchange (PBX)
    D. Domestic export

KEY (CORRECT ANSWERS)

1.	B		11.	D
2.	A		12.	C
3.	B		13.	D
4.	C		14.	B
5.	C		15.	D
6.	D		16.	C
7.	C		17.	C
8.	D		18.	A
9.	D		19.	C
10.	A		20.	B

21. D
22. C
23. D
24. A
25. B

TEST 2

DIRECTIONS: Each question or incomplete statement is followed by several suggested answers or completions. Select the one that BEST answers the question or completes the statement. *PRINT THE LETTER OF THE CORRECT ANSWER IN THE SPACE AT THE RIGHT.*

1. *Intelligent agent* software is an appropriate tool for each of the following applications EXCEPT

    A. finding cheap airfares
    B. conducting data conferences
    C. scheduling appointments
    D. deleting junk e-mail

1.____

2. Which of the following is the general term for high-speed digital communications networks that are national or worldwide in scope and accessible by the general public?

    A. Wide-area networks (WANs)
    B. Internet
    C. World Wide Web
    D. Information superhighway

2.____

3. Which of the following types of organizations is LEAST likely to make use of a hierarchical database?

    A. Insurance companies
    B. Consultancies/service organizations
    C. Banks
    D. National retailers

3.____

4. A transmission rate of _____ per second falls within the normal range for a local-area network.

    A. 70 bits   B. 100 kilobits
    C. 100 megabits   D. 3 gigabits

4.____

5. In the history of artificial intelligence, the effort to build a physical analog to the human brain has been referred to as the _____ approach.

    A. schematic   B. sequential
    C. neuronet   D. bottom-up

5.____

6. In an individual MIS, the most commonly-used technique for conducting operations research is _____ programming.

    A. productivity   B. statistical
    C. management   D. linear

6.____

7. Of the types of organizational change that are enabled by information technology, which tends to be the most common?

    A. Paradigm shift
    B. Automation
    C. Business reengineering
    D. Rationalization of procedures

7.____

8. Which of the following is offered the clearest protection under the Electronic Communications Privacy Act of 1986?

    A. Personal e-mail received from outside by the organization's system
    B. Interoffice fax transmissions
    C. Business-related phone calls received from outside by the organization's system
    D. Interoffice e-mail

8.__

9. Which of the following systems exists at the operational level of an organization?

    A. Transaction processing system (TPS)
    B. Executive support system (ESS)
    C. Office automation system (OAS)
    D. Management information system (MIS)

9.__

10. The representation of data as they appear to an application programmer or end user is described as a(n) _____ view.

    A. schematic   B. analogous
    C. logical   D. physical

10.__

11. Which of the computer hardware *generations* involved vacuum tube technology?

    A. First   B. Second   C. Third   D. Fourth

11.__

12. Which of the following is an example of the administrative message switching application of telecommunications technology?

    A. Inventory control
    B. Electronic mail
    C. Library systems
    D. International transfer of bank funds

12.__

13. Which of the following styles of systems development is most often used for information systems at the enterprise level?

    A. Prototyping   B. Outsourcing
    C. End-user development   D. Traditional life cycle

13.__

14. Which of the following is an element of the physical design of an information system?

    A. Manual procedures   B. Input descriptions
    C. Processing functions   D. Controls

14.__

15. Which of the following functions to connect dissimilar networks by providing the translation from one protocol to another?

    A. Gateway   B. Assembler   C. Gopher   D. Buffer

15.__

16. The primary memory of most microcomputers is measured in

    A. megabytes   B. gigabytes   C. kilobytes   D. bytes

16.__

17. _____ tools is a project management technique that structures and sequences tasks, and budgets the time, money, and technical resources required to complete these tasks.

    A. Internal integration   B. Formal control
    C. External integration   D. Formal planning

17.__

18. What is the term for the capacity of a communications channel as measured by the difference between the highest and lowest frequencies that can be transmitted by that channel?

    A. Transmissivity   B. Broadband
    C. Baud rate   D. Bandwidth

18.____

19. Which of the following are LEAST likely to be an input into a management information system (MIS)?

    A. Design specifications   B. Simple models
    C. Summary transaction data D. High-volume data

19.____

20. Which of the following is a shared network service technology that packages data into bundles for transmission but does not use error correction routines?

    A. Private branch exchange   B. Packet switching
    C. Internal integration   D. Frame relay

20.____

21. A purpose of a file server in a network is to

    A. collect messages for batch transmission
    B. route communications
    C. store programs
    D. connect dissimilar networks

21.____

22. _____ testing provides the final certification that a new system is ready to be used in a production setting.

    A. Parallel   B. Unit
    C. Acceptance   D. System

22.____

23. The number of _____ is NOT an example of software metrics.

    A. payroll checks printed per hour
    B. known users who are dissatisfied with an application's performance
    C. transactions that can be processed in one business day
    D. known bugs per hundred lines of code

23.____

24. What is the term for a set or rules that govern the manipulation of characters in a system?

    A. Synergy   B. Entropy
    C. Aggregation   D. Calculus

24.____

25. During the process of enterprise analysis, the results of a large managerial survey are broken down into each of the following EXCEPT

    A. processes   B. goals
    C. data matrices   D. functions

25.____

KEY (CORRECT ANSWERS)

1.	B	11.	A
2.	D	12.	B
3.	B	13.	D
4.	C	14.	A
5.	D	15.	A
6.	D	16.	C
7.	B	17.	D
8.	A	18.	D
9.	A	19.	A
10.	C	20.	D

21.	C
22.	C
23.	B
24.	D
25.	B

———

EXAMINATION SECTION
TEST 1

DIRECTIONS: Each question or incomplete statement is followed by several suggested answers or completions. Select the one that BEST answers the question or completes the statement. *PRINT THE LETTER OF THE CORRECT ANSWER IN THE SPACE AT THE RIGHT.*

1. Knowledge work systems are most typically used by each of the following personnel EXCEPT
   1.____

   A. middle managers
   B. salespeople
   C. engineers
   D. accountants

2. A media-oriented description of a system's operations is BEST represented by a(n)
   2.____

   A. systems flowchart
   B. system requirements plan
   C. Gantt chart
   D. program flowchart

3. During preliminary analysis, a feasibility group will study the three fundamental operations of an existing system.
   Which of the following is NOT one of these operations?
   3.____

   A. Output of information
   B. Data processing
   C. Coding
   D. Data preparation and input

4. Normally, the starting point of any systems design is to determine the
   4.____

   A. output
   B. hardware
   C. throughput
   D. users

5. From its beginnings, the total time required for an entire systems analysis and design process to be completed will MOST likely be
   5.____

   A. 6-12 months
   B. 12-18 months
   C. 2-3 years
   D. 3-5 years

6. In a data flow diagram, a square like the one shown at the right would be used to represent
   6.____

   A. input to the system
   B. a terminal
   C. magnetic tape
   D. a display

7. A _____ systems conversion takes place when the old system is switched off and the new one is started up.
   7.____

   A. day-one   B. direct   C. parallel   D. pilot

8. The MOST common reason for the failure of an information system is
   8.____

   A. faulty programming
   B. hardware obsolescence
   C. interface complications
   D. faulty problem identification

9. A personnel record in a master file consists of the following fields, containing the indi-   9.___
   cated number of characters.

Field	Number of Characters
Identication number	5
Social Security number	9
Name	25
Address	35
Sex	2
Code number	1

   If the master file contains 2,000 transactions, then approximately how many characters
   would the file be expected to hold?
   A. 56,000   B.   115,500   C.   154,000   D.   231,000

10. Which of the following is NOT one of the primary elements of a data flow diagram?   10.___

   A.   Process   B.   External entity
   C.   Rule number   D.   Data store

11. During systems design, each of the following is a consideration involving input EXCEPT   11.___

   A.   media   B.   validity checking
   C.   volume   D.   security

12. The MAIN advantage involved with the use of pilot systems conversion is   12.___

   A.   speed of conversion process
   B.   provides constant backup media
   C.   makes file conversion unnecessary
   D.   minimizes problems by confining operations

13. _____ is NOT a type of systems control.   13.___

   A.   Auditing   B.   Contingency planning
   C.   Data security   D.   Data control

14. In a _____ type of systems conversion, various capabilities are added to the system   14.___
   over a number of years.

   A.   graduated   B.   pilot   C.   phased   D.   indirect

15. Which of the following is NOT a standard classification for a system in terms of cost-   15.___
   effectiveness?

   A.   Risky   B.   Safe
   C.   Pioneering   D.   Prudent

16. _____ accounts for the GREATEST expenditure involved in the cost of creating and   16.___
   maintaining a system.

   A.   Systems design
   B.   Equipment
   C.   Evaluation and maintenance
   D.   Implementation

17. Which of the following is NOT one of the procedures involved in program development?   17.____

    A. Program preparation   B. Systems audit evaluation
    C. Scheduling   D. Testing

18. The PRIMARY purpose of the systems analysis phase of the entire analysis and design   18.____
process is to

    A. compose an accurate data flow diagram
    B. determine input, output, and processing requirements
    C. determine whether to modify the existing system or convert completely to a new
        one
    D. consider the people who will be interacting with the new system

19. Which of the following is NOT a major problem associated with systems building?   19.____

    A. Coordination costs   B. Hardware currency
    C. Requirements analysis   D. Record keeping

20. Typically, a workable system is the output of the _____ phase of systems analysis and   20.____
design.

    A. systems development   B. systems analysis
    C. systems design   D. implementation

21. The MOST reliable means of obtaining information about an existing system can be   21.____
obtained through the use of

    A. observations   B. personal interviews
    C. questionnaires   D. written forms

22. The purpose of a printer spacing chart is to   22.____

    A. represent the exact format of a system's output
    B. assist in data validity checking
    C. coordinate all related fields into a single report
    D. describe the input data needed to produce the system's output

23. The FIRST procedure in a system test plan is usually _____ testing.   23.____

    A. crash proof   B. system
    C. personnel   D. unit

24. The cost-benefit analysis of a proposed system is USUALLY performed during the   24.____
_____ phase of analysis and design.

    A. systems design   B. systems analysis
    C. preliminary analysis   D. implementation

25. The MOST significant output of the systems analysis phase of the entire analysis and   25.____
design process is the

    A. detailed system design
    B. system requirements plan
    C. installed and operational system
    D. preliminary plan

KEY (CORRECT ANSWERS)

1.	B	11.	D
2.	A	12.	D
3.	C	13.	A
4.	A	14.	C
5.	C	15.	A
6.	A	16.	D
7.	B	17.	B
8.	D	18.	C
9.	C	19.	B
10.	C	20.	A

21.	B
22.	A
23.	D
24.	A
25.	B

TEST 2

DIRECTIONS: Each question or incomplete statement is followed by several suggested answers or completions. Select the one that BEST answers the question or completes the statement. *PRINT THE LETTER OF THE CORRECT ANSWER IN THE SPACE AT THE RIGHT.*

1. Systems maintenance involves three important factors that are considered during the design and development phases of a project. Which of the following is NOT one of these three?

   A. Structured programming
   B. System documentation
   C. System auditing
   D. Anticipation of future needs

   1._____

2. In a data flow diagram, an open-ended rectangle like the one shown at the right would be used to represent

   A. an invoice   B. a punched card
   C. data storage   D. data preparation

   2._____

3. Systems design reports normally include each of the following EXCEPT a(n)

   A. review of the problems associated with the present system
   B. overview of the proposed system
   C. summation of the major findings of the cost-benefit analysis
   D. list of hardware recommended for the proposed system

   3._____

4. A _____ group is NOT usually involved in a typical systems project team.

   A. vendor   B. user
   C. management   D. programming

   4._____

5. The _____ method of systems conversion is typically the riskiest.

   A. parallel   B. pilot   C. day-one   D. direct

   5._____

6. The PRIMARY purpose of a decision table used in systems analysis is to

   A. describe the sequence of operations that must be performed to obtain a computer solution to a problem
   B. represent all the combinations of conditions that must be satisfied before an action can be taken
   C. describe the operations to be performed by the system, with a major emphasis on the media involved, as well as the workstations through which they pass
   D. graphically depict the flow of data and the processes that change or transform data throughout the system

   6._____

7. Which of the following is used to describe a system's necessary input data?

   A. Systems flowchart   B. CRT layout form
   C. Data flow diagram   D. Record layout form

   7._____

8. The LONGEST phase involved in the systems analysis and design process is the _____ phase.

    A. implementation   B. systems design
    C. systems development   D. preliminary analysis

8.__

9. The systems development phase of analysis and design normally includes each of the following EXCEPT

    A. purchase of equipment   B. program testing
    C. user training   D. program development

9.__

10. In cases where it is too expensive to convert a system's old files and applications, a(n) _____ system conversion is commonly used.

    A. parallel   B. pilot   C. direct   D. day-one

10.__

11. The PRIMARY purpose of an audit trail is to

    A. trace specific input data to its related output
    B. error-check a new systems program
    C. locate workstations where unauthorized users are at work
    D. check data validity

11.__

12. A system requirements plan typically includes each of the following EXCEPT

    A. description of how existing system works
    B. hardware requirements for the new system
    C. information necessary for the new system
    D. major problems of existing system

12.__

13. A _____ is typically a member of the programming group of a systems project team.

    A. vendor   B. user
    C. management   D. librarian

13.__

14. The implementation phase of systems analysis and design does NOT usually include

    A. training   B. auditing
    C. programming   D. system conversion

14.__

15. The _____ is a document created by the systems project team that takes into account the organizational constraints and the personnel involved in using a new system.

    A. system requirements report
    B. statement of objectives
    C. test plan
    D. request for proposal

15.__

16. Which of the following is used as an aid to scheduling system operations?

    A. Gantt chart   B. Circle graph
    C. Chief programmer   D. Head node

16.__

17. The MAIN disadvantage associated with parallel systems conversion is that   17._____

    A. it usually takes more time than all other approaches
    B. there is costly duplication of personnel efforts and equipment
    C. confusion is involved in constant switch-overs
    D. no backup is provided

18. Transaction processing systems are LEAST likely to be used by   18._____

    A. knowledge professionals
    B. data entry specialists
    C. customers
    D. clerks

19. When a new system is used in its entirety only in one locality or area, _____ is being   19._____
practiced.

    A. batch processing   B. live data analysis
    C. pilot conversion   D. file conversion

20. Which of the following is NOT a software tool that has been developed to help a systems   20._____
analyst build better systems in a more timely and cost-effective manner?

    A. CAD tools   B. Project management tools
    C. Prototyping   D. CASE tools

21. Action stubs and conditions entries are components of the   21._____

    A. program flowchart   B. decision table
    C. system flowchart   D. Gantt chart

22. When both an old and a new system are run simultaneously for a period of time to   22._____
ensure the new system's proper operation, _____ is being practiced.

    A. incremental auditing   B. file conversion
    C. parallel conversion   D. direct switch-over

23. The FIRST operation performed during the implementation phase of analysis and design   23._____
is usually

    A. file conversion   B. systems evaluation
    C. systems conversion   D. auditing

24. Typically, programming accounts for _____% of the hours spent on systems analysis   24._____
and design.

    A. 10   B. 20   C. 35   D. 45

25. In a data flow diagram, a circle like the one shown at the right would be used to   25._____
represent

    A. output from the system
    B. a single file
    C. a manual action
    D. a process that transforms data in some way

KEY (CORRECT ANSWERS)

1.	C		11.	A
2.	C		12.	B
3.	D		13.	D
4.	A		14.	C
5.	D		15.	B
6.	B		16.	A
7.	D		17.	B
8.	C		18.	A
9.	C		19.	C
10.	D		20.	A

21. B
22. C
23. A
24. B
25. D

EXAMINATION SECTION
TEST 1

DIRECTIONS: Each question or incomplete statement is followed by several suggested answers or completions. Select the one that BEST answers the question or completes the statement. *PRINT THE LETTER OF THE CORRECT ANSWER IN THE SPACE AT THE RIGHT.*

1. The analysis phase of the systems process is divided into

    A. preliminary and detailed
    B. input and output
    C. hardware and software
    D. costs and benefits
    E. people and procedures

1.____

2. Detailed analysis involves

    A. an investigation of the existing system
    B. how an organization collects data
    C. how an organization processes data
    D. how to improve the processing of data
    E. all of the above

2.____

3. When conducting the detailed analysis, the analyst consults with

    A. users
    B. outside vendors
    C. management
    D. other members of the computing services staff
    E. all of the above

3.____

4. Before starting the detailed analysis, the analyst reviews the

    A. organization chart   B. preliminary report
    C. database design   D. screen lay-out formats
    E. program specifications

4.____

5. An output from analysis is the

    A. program specifications
    B. module specifications
    C. input data collection screen designs
    D. feasibility study
    E. database design

5.____

6. The FIRST task in detailed analysis is

    A. fact-finding
    B. presentation of analysis to management
    C. review and assignment
    D. interviewing users
    E. none of the above

6.____

7. The LAST task in detailed analysis is

    A. fact-finding
    B. presentation of analysis to management
    C. review and assignment
    D. interviewing users
    E. none of the above

7.___

8. A tool an analyst can use to assist in scheduling is the

    A. data flow diagram   B. Gantt chart
    C. Warnier-Orr diagram   D. CPM chart
    E. HIPO chart

8.___

9. In a Gantt chart, events are listed

    A. as bars
    B. as rectangles
    C. along the left-hand side
    D. along the right-hand side
    E. across the bottom

9.___

10. In a Gantt chart personnel assigned to events are listed

    A. as bars
    B. as rectangles
    C. along the left-hand side
    D. along the right-hand side
    E. across the bottom

10.___

11. As tasks are completed, the analyst updates the Gantt chart by

    A. filling in hollow horizontal bars
    B. completing a worksheet
    C. reviewing the task assignments
    D. notifying management
    E. none of the above

11.___

12. Fact-finding means an analyst needs to

    A. learn as much as possible about the system
    B. interview all company personnel
    C. review the systems study
    D. review the program specifications
    E. talk with hardware vendors

12.___

13. Which one of the following is NOT a part of the four W's the analyst must ask?

    A. Who is involved?
    B. What do you do?
    C. While you do it, what are others doing?
    D. Why do you do it the way you do?
    E. When do you do it?

13.___

14. Users should be notified of the detailed analysis by   14.____

    A. telephone call
    B. general meeting
    C. a memorandum
    D. a notice in the company newsletter
    E. a meeting at the water fountain

15. During fact-finding, the analyst gathers together   15.____

    A. forms
    B. documents
    C. interviews with key staff members
    D. observations of the system
    E. all of the above

16. Questions posed on a questionnaire should be   16.____

    A. worded using computer jargon
    B. lead the responder to draw conclusions
    C. nonthreatening
    D. vague
    E. general purpose

17. Which type of questionnaire gives respondents a specific set of potential answers?   17.____

    A. Open-ended   B. Multiple choice
    C. Rating   D. Rank
    E. None of the above

18. Which type of questionnaire gives respondents a chance to answer in their own words?   18.____

    A. Open-ended   B. Multiple choice
    C. Rating   D. Rank
    E. None of the above

19. Which type of questionnaire gives respondents a chance to show their satisfaction?   19.____

    A. Open-ended   B. Multiple choice
    C. Rating   D. Rank
    E. None of the above

20. Which type of questionnaire gives respondents a chance to prioritize on a high to low basis?   20.____

    A. Open-ended   B. Multiple choice
    C. Rating   D. Rank
    E. None of the above

KEY (CORRECT ANSWERS)

1.	A	11.	A
2.	E	12.	A
3.	E	13.	C
4.	B	14.	C
5.	D	15.	E
6.	C	16.	C
7.	B	17.	B
8.	B	18.	A
9.	C	19.	C
10.	E	20.	D

TEST 2

DIRECTIONS: Each question or incomplete statement is followed by several suggested answers or completions. Select the one that BEST answers the question or completes the statement. *PRINT THE LETTER OF THE CORRECT ANSWER IN THE SPACE AT THE RIGHT.*

1. When observing an existing system, an analyst should be

    1._____

    A. an observer
    B. a questioner
    C. a part of the system
    D. an answerer
    E. making value judgments

2. When observing a system, it is LIKELY that the system will

    2._____

    A. not function
    B. operate 500% faster
    C. operate 50% slower
    D. operate differently than it normally does
    E. none of the above

3. After observing the system, the analyst can draw a diagram of the logical system using which of the following techniques?

    3._____

    A. Data flow diagram
    B. Gantt chart
    C. HIPO chart
    D. PERT chart
    E. IPD chart

4. A data flow diagram that shows a system in its MOST general form is called a(n) _____ DFD.

    4._____

    A. analysis
    B. context
    C. levelled
    D. decomposed
    E. system

5. A data flow diagram that shows a system in its MOST specific form is called a(n) _____ DFD.

    5._____

    A. analysis
    B. context
    C. levelled
    D. decomposed
    E. system

6. To draw a DFD, the analyst should

    6._____

    A. identify activities
    B. isolate data flows
    C. look for duplication of data flows
    D. show the relationship between activities
    E. all of the above

7. An alternative that should ALWAYS be considered is

    7._____

    A. computerize the process
    B. program the process
    C. do nothing
    D. contract the process to outsiders
    E. all of the above

8. In deciding what to do, the analyst should consider

    A. costs   B. benefits   C. alternatives
    D. personnel   E. all of the above

8.___

9. In deciding what to do, the analyst should consider

    A. buying a packaged solution
    B. buying a main-frame computer
    C. hiring additional staff
    D. contracting the solution to an outside organization
    E. none of the above

9.___

10. The final report of findings produced during analysis is called

    A. the systems study
    B. the feasibility study
    C. the program study
    D. the programming specifications
    E. none of the above

10.___

11. The final report of findings is reviewed by

    A. management   B. users
    C. computer services staff   D. the analyst
    E. all of the above

11.___

12. The final report of findings is approved by

    A. management   B. users
    C. computer services staff   D. the analyst
    E. all of the above

12.___

13. If a recommendation is made to buy software from an outside supplier, the analyst should ask the supplier about

    A. cost and performance
    B. security and compatability
    C. upgrading and updates
    D. training and support
    E. all of the above

13.___

14. Future costs for a system should be

    A. added together
    B. ignored
    C. discounted
    D. subtracted from current costs
    E. all of the above

14.___

15. Besides costs, the analyst needs to calculate

    A. future needs
    B. benefits
    C. the impact on competitors

15.___

D. the impact on users
E. alternative messages

16. Which of the following costs MUST be considered in any alternative?   16.____

A. System design   B. System development
C. Hardware   D. Software and training
E. All of the above

17. When collecting documents for an accounts payable system, which is NOT appropriate?   17.____

A. Invoice   B. Packing slip
C. Monthly statement   D. Check
E. All are appropriate

18. Who should sign the analysis authorization memorandum?   18.____

A. The analyst   B. A manager   C. A user
D. A programmer   E. Any of the above

19. An output from analysis is the   19.____

A. program specifications
B. module specifications
C. input data collection screen designs
D. analysis documentation
E. database design

20. During interviews, an analyst functions like a(n)   20.____

A. newspaper reporter   B. architect
C. programmer   D. supervisor
E. friend or co-worker

_____

KEY (CORRECT ANSWERS)

1.	A		11.	E
2.	D		12.	A
3.	A		13.	E
4.	B		14.	C
5.	A		15.	B
6.	E		16.	E
7.	C		17.	C
8.	E		18.	B
9.	A		19.	D
10.	B		20.	A

_____

EXAMINATION SECTION
TEST 1

DIRECTIONS: Each question or incomplete statement is followed by several suggested answers or completions. Select the one that BEST answers the question or completes the statement. *PRINT THE LETTER OF THE CORRECT ANSWER IN THE SPACE AT THE RIGHT.*

1. _____ is commonly used to report on project performance.

    A. Earned Value Management
    B. WBS
    C. Quality Management Plan
    D. RBS

1._____

2. Which of the following is NOT a process associated with communications management?

    A. Distribute information
    B. Manage stakeholder expectations
    C. Plan communication
    D. Survey questionnaire

2._____

3. As a project manager, you are expected to make relevant information available to project stakeholders as planned. Which process does this relate to?

    A. Distribute information
    B. Manage stakeholder expectations
    C. Plan communication
    D. Report performance

3._____

4. Report performance involves all of the following EXCEPT

    A. collecting and distributing performance data
    B. collecting and distributing progress measurements
    C. collecting stakeholder information needs
    D. collecting and distributing forecasts

4._____

5. Of the following examples listed, which is a sign of feedback from the receiver?

    A. No written response from the receiver
    B. An acknowledgement or additional questions from the receiver
    C. Encoding the message by the receiver
    D. Decoding the message by the receiver

5._____

6. As a project manager you are expected to create a scope statement. Once you have the statement, you find it to be useful in all the following ways EXCEPT

    A. describing the purpose of the project
    B. describing the objectives of the project
    C. distributing information
    D. explaining the business problems the project is expected to solve

6._____

7. What are project deliverables?   7._____
   A. Tangible products that the project is expected to deliver
   B. Prioritized list of deliverables
   C. Project scope statement
   D. Project documents

8. As a project manager, you are arranging criteria for project completion criteria.   8._____
   You could organize it using all of the following EXCEPT
   A. functional department
   B. milestones
   C. tasks of projects
   D. project phase

9. Which of the following is not a task under "Developing human resource plan"?   9._____
   A. Documenting organizational relationships
   B. Looking for the availability of required human resources
   C. Identification and documentation of project roles and responsibilities
   D. Creating a staffing plan

10. If you are a project manager who is keen in managing a project team, you would   10._____
    undertake any of the following EXCEPT
    A. creating a staffing plan
    B. evaluating individual team member performance
    C. providing feedback
    D. resolving conflicts

11. Nurturing the team is a vital role of a project manager. If you have to do so, what   11._____
    would you avoid?
    A. Guide the team members as required
    B. Provide mentoring throughout the project
    C. Remove the team member who is found to be less skilled
    D. On-the-job training

12. War room creation is an example of   12._____
    A. co-location
    B. management skills
    C. rewards and recognitions
    D. establishing ground rules

13. The team member roles and responsibilities could be documented using all of the   13._____
    following EXCEPT
    A. functional chart
    B. text-oriented format
    C. hierarchical type organizational chart
    D. matrix-based responsibility chart

14. _____ is NOT an example of constraints placed upon the project by current organizational policies.

    A. Hiring freeze
    B. Reduced training funds
    C. Organizational chart templates
    D. Rewards and Increments Freeze

    14._____

15. As a project manager, you have decided to have a virtual team. What kind of limitation would this create with regards to team development?

    A. Rewards and recognition
    B. Establishing ground rules
    C. Team building
    D. Co-location

    15._____

16. Unplanned training means

    A. team building using virtual team arrangement
    B. competencies developed as a result of project performance appraisals
    C. on-the-job training
    D. training that is done without any planning in advance

    16._____

17. Resource break down structure is an example of

    A. functional chart
    B. text-oriented format
    C. hierarchical type organizational chart
    D. matrix-based responsibility chart

    17._____

18. A project manager would consider the following as inputs to define scope EXCEPT

    A. requirements document
    B. project Charter
    C. product management plan
    D. organizational process charts

    18._____

19. Aldo is a project manager and has to terminate a project earlier than planned. The level and extent of completion should be documented. Under which is this done?

    A. Verify scope
    B. Create scope
    C. Control scope
    D. Define scope

    19._____

20. Sam, an IT project manager, is having difficulty in getting resources for his project, and hence has to depend highly on department heads. Which type of organization is Sam most likely working with?

    A. Functional
    B. Tight matrix
    C. Weak matrix
    D. Projectized

    20._____

Questions 21-25.

Len is a project manager of an infrastructure project manager of a well-known company. He is involved in various processes of scope management. Look at the following chart and align the different processes to various tasks listed. Choose the appropriate answer for each process and list them under corresponding tasks.

	Processes	Corresponding tasks	List of tasks
21.	Define scope	21._____	A. Monitoring project scope and project status
22.	Control scope	22._____	B. Defining and documenting stakeholder needs
23.	Collect requirements	23._____	C. Formalizing acceptance of the complete project deliverables
24.	Verify scope	24._____	D. Breaking down the project into smaller, more manageable tasks
25.	Create WBS	25._____	E. Developing a detailed description of the project and its ultimate product

---

KEY (CORRECT ANSWERS)

1. A	11. C	21. E
2. D	12. A	22. A
3. A	13. A	23. B
4. C	14. C	24. C
5. B	15. D	25. D
6. C	16. B	
7. A	17. C	
8. C	18. C	
9. B	19. A	
10. A	20. A	

TEST 2

DIRECTIONS: Each question or incomplete statement is followed by several suggested answers or completions. Select the one that BEST answers the question or completes the statement. *PRINT THE LETTER OF THE CORRECT ANSWER IN THE SPACE AT THE RIGHT.*

1. In which of the following processes would risk be identified?
   A. Risk identification
   B. Risk monitoring and control
   C. Qualitative risk analysis
   D. Risk identification, monitoring and control

   1._____

2. Jack has prepared a risk management plan for his project and also identified risks in his project. Which of the following processes should Jack do next?
   A. Plan risk responses
   B. Perform qualitative analysis
   C. Perform quantitative analysis
   D. Monitor and control risk

   2._____

3. Which of the following is NOT a step in risk management?
   A. Perform qualitative analysis
   B. Monitor and control risk
   C. Risk identification
   D. Risk breakdown structure

   3._____

4. Sue is a project manager for an IT project at a corporate office. She is engaged in the process of identifying risks. To do so, she collects inputs from experts from the field through a questionnaire. What is this technique called?
   A. Interview
   B. Documentation review
   C. Delphi technique
   D. Register risk

   4._____

5. Positive risks may be responded by which of the following:
   I. Exploit   II. Accept   III. Mitigate   IV. Share

   A. I and III
   B. All of the above
   C. I, II and IV
   D. I, II and III

   5._____

6. Risk _____ is a response to negative risks.
   A. identification
   B. mitigation
   C. response plan
   D. management plan

   6._____

7. Which of the following statements is NOT true about risk management?   7._____
   A. Risk register documents all the risks in detail
   B. Risks always have negative impacts and not positive
   C. Risk mitigation is a response to negative risks
   D. Risk register documents the risks in detail

8. _____ is the document that lists all the risks in a hierarchical fashion.   8._____
   A. Risk breakdown structure
   B. Lists of risks
   C. Risk management plan
   D. Monte Carlo diagram

9. Nicole is a project manager of a reforestation project. In one of the project   9._____
   reviews, she realizes that a risk has occurred. Which document should Nicole
   refer to take an appropriate action?
   A. Risk response plan
   B. Risk register
   C. Risk management plan
   D. Risk breakdown structure

10. As a project manager, you have invited experts for an effective brainstorming   10._____
    session to identify risks involved in the project. What is the ideal group size?
    A. 3   B. 6   C. 4   D. 5

11. Of the following personnel, who is NOT involved in project risk identification   11._____
    activities?
    A. Clerical staff
    B. Subject matter experts
    C. Other project managers
    D. Risk management experts

12. _____ is one of the tools/techniques used in risk identification.   12._____
    A. Risk tracker
    B. Checklist analysis
    C. Risk register
    D. Project scope

13. Jim is a project manager in a bank. He is collecting input for the risk   13._____
    identification process. What input would he be collecting to identify risks?
        I.   Project scope statement
        II. Enterprise environmental factors
        III. Project management plan
        IV. Diagramming techniques

    A. I and IV only
    B. III and IV only
    C. All of the above
    D. I, II and III only

14. Which of the following could a project manager collect from a risk tracker?
   I.   Root causes of risk and updated risk categories
   II.   List of identified risks
   III.   Risk register
   IV.   List of potential responses

  A.   I and IV only
  B.   III and IV only
  C.   I, II and IV
  D.   II only

14._____

15. The risk management plan should describe the entire risk management process, including auditing of the process, and should also define _____.
  A.   reporting
  B.   environmental factors
  C.   organizational process assets
  D.   project management plan

15._____

16. What do risk categories define?
  A.   How to communicate risk activities and their results
  B.   Types and sources of risks
  C.   How risk management will be done on the process
  D.   When and how the risk management activities appear in the project schedule

16._____

17. Which of the following is not a method of risk identification?
  A.   Diagramming
  B.   Interviewing
  C.   SWOT
  D.   RBS

17._____

18. Shauna is conducting a qualitative risk analysis for her project. What is she required to do?
  A.   Apply a numerical rating to each risk
  B.   Assess the probability and impact of each identified risk
  C.   Assign each major risk to a risk owner
  D.   Outline a course of action for each major risk identified

18._____

19. Which of the following is not a criterion to close a risk?
  A.   Risk is no longer valid
  B.   Risk event has occurred
  C.   Risk activities are recorded regularly
  D.   Risk closure at the direction of a project manager

19._____

20. As a project manager, you establish a risk contingency budget. Which of the following is not a purpose of establishing a risk contingency budget?
    A. To be reviewed as a standing agenda item for project team meetings
    B. To prepare in advance to manage the risks successfully
    C. To have some reserve funds
    D. To avoid going over the budget allotted

20._____

21. Which of the following statements is NOT correct in terms of designing a risk management?
    A. Risk is inherent to project work
    B. In any organization, projects will have common risks
    C. Some risks may occur more than once in the life a project
    D. Risks identified will definitely occur

21._____

22. All identified potential risk events that are viewed to be relevant to the project are to be recorded using the
    A. risk register
    B. risk management matrix
    C. risk report
    D. SOW

22._____

23. _____ is/are an example of a business risk.
    A. Poorly understood requirements
    B. A merger
    C. Introduction of new technology to the organization
    D. Work outside the project scope

23._____

24. Personnel turnover in a project is a
    A. Business risk
    B. Not a risk at all
    C. Technology risk
    D. Project risk

24._____

25. Which of the following is not an example of mitigation?
    A. Set expectations
    B. Involve customer in early planning process
    C. Provide training for personnel
    D. Hiring a backup person for a key team member

25._____

_____

KEY (CORRECT ANSWERS)

1. D
2. B
3. D
4. C
5. C

6. B
7. B
8. A
9. A
10. A

11. A
12. B
13. D
14. C
15. A

16. B
17. D
18. B
19. C
20. A

21. D
22. B
23. B
24. D
25. D

———————

TEST 3

DIRECTIONS: Each question or incomplete statement is followed by several suggested answers of completions. Select the one that best answers the question or complete the statement. *PRINT THE LETTER OF THE CORRECT ANSWER IN THE SPACE AT THE RIGHT.*

1. Project cost management deals with all the following EXCEPT: 1._
   A. Estimating costs
   B. Budgeting
   C. Controlling costs
   D. Communicating costs

2. Which of the following is not a process associated with project cost management?   2._
   A. Control costs
   B. Maintain reserves
   C. Estimate costs
   D. Determine budget

3. _____ is not a key deliverable of project cost processes.   3._
   A. Cost performance baseline
   B. Activity cost estimates
   C. Results of estimates
   D. Work performance measurements

4. As a project manager, you are calculating depreciation for an object. You are doing this by depreciating the same amount from the cost each year.   4._
   What kind of depreciation technique are you applying?
   A. Sum of year depreciation
   B. Double-declining balance
   C. Multiple depreciation
   D. Straight line depreciation

5. Which of the following is not a characteristic of analogous estimating?   5._
   A. It is a top-down approach
   B. It is a form of an expert judgment
   C. It makes less time when compared to bottom-up estimation
   D. It is more accurate when compared to bottom-up estimation

6. CPI = EV/AC. If CPI is less than 1, the project   6._
   A. is over the budget
   B. is within the budget
   C. would be left over with unused budget
   D. efficiency is less

7. Which of the following is not a tool used for estimating cost?   7._
   A. Cost of quality
   B. Expert judgment
   C. Two point estimates
   D. Three point estimates

8. What are the traditional project management triple constraints?   8._
   A. Time, cost, resources
   B. Scope, cost, resources
   C. Scope, time, cost
   D. Resources, scope, budget

9. Sam, an IT project manager, is having difficulty getting resources for his project, and hence has to depend highly on department heads.
   Which type of organization is Sam most likely working with?
   A. Functional
   B. Tight Matrix
   C. Weak Matrix
   D. Projectized

9._____

10. After-project costs are called _____.
    A. cost of quality
    B. extra costs
    C. life cycle costs
    D. over budget costs

10._____

11. Critical chain is a tool and technique for _____.
    A. developing schedule process
    B. defining critical path
    C. sequencing activities process
    D. estimating activity duration

11._____

12. The following are outputs for sequencing activities:
    A. Project schedule network diagram, Milestone list
    B. Project document updates, Project schedule network diagram
    C. Project schedule, Project document updates
    D. Schedule data, Schedule baseline

12._____

13. The schedule performance index is a measure of:
    A. Difference between earned value and planned value
    B. Ratio between earned value and planned value
    C. Difference between earned value and estimate at completion
    D. Ratio between estimate at completion and earned value

13._____

14. Which of the following is not an input, output or tools and technique for control schedule process?
    A. Project schedule, work performance measurements and variance analysis
    B. Project management plan, project document updates and schedule compression
    C. Work performance information, schedule baseline and schedule data
    D. Project schedule, change requests and resource leveling

14._____

15. Contracts, resource calendar, risk register and forecasts are all termed as
    A. inputs to administer procurements process
    B. outputs from close procurements process
    C. project documents
    D. tools and techniques of conduct procurement process

15._____

16. Fast tracking can be best described as
    A. one of the schedule compression techniques
    B. adding resources to activities on critical path
    C. shared or critical resources available only at specific times
    D. performing activities in parallel to shorten project duration

16._____

17. Which of the following contract types places the highest risk on the seller?   17._
    A. Cost plus fixed fee
    B. Firm fixed price
    C. Cost plus incentive fee
    D. Time and material

18. Using the Power/Interest grid, a stakeholder with low power and having high interest on   18._
    the project should be
    A. monitored
    B. managed closely
    C. kept satisfied
    D. kept informed

19. Stakeholder classification information is found in which of the following documents?   19._
    A. Communications management plan
    B. Stakeholder register
    C. Stakeholder management strategy document
    D. Human resource plan

20. Thomas is a project manager of a well-reputed organization. One of your senior   20._
    managers approaches you to explain constraints on labor utilization followed by a
    request to delay a couple of your projects. What is the best way to approach this
    situation?
    A. Agree with the senior manager and delay a couple of your projects
    B. Perform an impact analysis of the requested change
    C. Report the situation to the senior management and make a complaint against the
       senior manager
    D. Disagree with the senior manager and continue with the progress of the projects
       managed by you

21. Project management is defined as   21._
    A. completion of a project
    B. gaining trust of the people involved in the project
    C. completing a WBS
    D. the application of specific knowledge, skills and tools

22. The most common form of dependency is   22._
    A. Start to Start
    B. Finish to Start
    C. Finish to Finish
    D. Start to Finish

23. Kelly is a project manager who is in phase of project evaluation. Which of the   23._
    following has to be considered during project evaluation phase?
    I.   Give feedback to team members
    II.   Learn from experiences
    III. Monitor
    IV.   Celebrate

The correct answer(s) is/are:
- A. I only
- B. I, IV and III
- C. III only
- D. I, II and IV

24. Which of the following are very vital for the implementation of the project, and also must be repeated over and over during project's life.

   I.   Correct
  II.   Monitor
 III. Estimate time and cost
 IV. Analyze

24._____

The correct answer(s) is/are:
- A. I, II and III
- B. III only
- C. I, III and IV
- D. I, II and IV

25. What is the average amount of time is to be allocated to project planning?

25._____

- A. 10%
- B. 25%
- C. 22%
- D. 2%

KEY (CORRECT ANSWERS)

1. D	11. A
2. B	12. B
3. C	13. B
4. C	14. C
5. D	15. C
6. A	16. D
7. C	17. B
8. C	18. D
9. A	19. B
10. C	20. B

21. D
22. B
23. D
24. D
25. A

TEST 4

Each question or incomplete statement is followed by several suggested answers of completions. Select the one that best answers the question or complete the statement. *PRINT THE LETTER OF THE CORRECT ANSWER IN THE SPACE AT THE RIGHT.*

1. Imagine you are assigned a project for which you do not have the required competency and experience to manage. What is the best plan of action?
    A. Make sure that you disclose any areas of improvement that need to be immediately addressed with the project sponsor before accepting the assignment
    B. Do not inform anyone about the gaps and learn as much as you can before any critical activity is due for delivery
    C. Consider the opportunity as a stepping stone for your career development and accept it
    D. Tell your boss that you cannot manage as you do not have the relevant experience and decline it

1.__

2. You are the project manager of a new project and are involved in selecting a vendor for acquiring products required for the project. Your close friend is running a company that is also very competitive and a reputed one along with other vendors who are competing for the bid. How can you handle this situation?
    A. Do not participate in the vendor selection process as this may be considered a conflict of interest
    B. Provide information to help your friend get the contract as you are the project manager of the project
    C. Do not inform anyone about your personal contact and be involved in the vendor selection process as normal
    D. Discuss with your project sponsor the possibility of a conflict of interest and leave the decision to him on the next steps

2.__

3. You have provided good guidance to your team members and this has resulted in successful execution of all of the phases involved. There was a particular phase that has been identified as very critical and the presence of a technical expert helped achieve this success. In the senior management review meeting you were credited with the success of the project, with specific mention of that particular phase. What do you do in this situation?
    A. Accept the appreciation and feel proud about the success of the project
    B. Do not mention anything about the technical expert role as you were the project manager for this project
    C. Give credit to the technical expert and let the senior management know how the presence of the technical expert helped the team to be successful
    D. Accept the appreciation from the senior management and thank the technical expert in private for achieving this success

3.__

4. As a project manager you are preparing status reports for a meeting with the stakeholders. 4._____
One of your team members has come out with an issue that will cause some delay in
the project timeline. You have a plan that can be implemented to make sure that this
issue can be managed without causing any delay in the timeline, but you currently
do not have the time to update the project plan. How will you handle this situation?
   - A. Present the status of the project as *on-track* without discussing anything about this
     issue as you will have time to prepare before the next meeting
   - B. Cancel the meeting as you do not have the time to update the details to be provided
     to the stakeholders
   - C. Present the status of the project *as-is* without minimizing the effect of the delay
     and discuss details of the planned approach to solve this issue
   - D. Fire your team that is responsible for causing this delay as it has created a bad
     impression of you amongst the stakeholders

5. John is an Associate Director in a pharmaceutical company managing its internal 5._____
projects. He has presented whitepapers on project execution methodologies and is
highly respected within the organization. He also regularly conducts workshops &
lectures in coordination with PMO. What kind of power does John possess?
   - A. Referent power
   - B. Coercive power
   - C. Reward power
   - D. Expert power

6. You are a project manager working for a non-profit organization. You had 6._____
been assigned a project that is in the initial stage and involves development of an
eco-system in a large community. You are reviewing the deliverables and templates
from similar projects that are available in the company lessons learnt knowledge base.
Which item will be of much importance to you?
   - A. Project Information Management System
   - B. Enterprise Environmental Factors
   - C. Organization Process Assets
   - D. Standard Templates

7. A project that you were managing is nearing completion. As part of the deliverables you 7._____
are required to complete lessons-learned documentation of the project. What is the
primary purpose of creating lessons-learned documentation?
   - A. Provide information of project success
   - B. Help identify all the failures
   - C. Provide information on minimizing negative impacts and maximizing positive
     events for future projects of similar nature
   - D. Comply with the organization's objectives

8. You are managing project teams that work from different locations and there has been 8._____
issues with the teams' ability to effectively perform. This has resulted in delay in timeline.
Which kind of team development technique would be most effective in this situation?
   - A. Mediation
   - B. Training
   - C. Co-location
   - D. Rewards

9. The project sponsor has requested that you create a project charter for a new project 9._____
that you will manage next month. Which document will you utilize to create the
project charter that will justify the need for the project?
   - A. Project SOW
   - B. Business Need
   - C. Business Case
   - D. Cost-benefit Analysis

10. An audit is being performed by a team for the project you are managing. 10.
The team reports that the standards utilized need to be analyzed as several
processes that are not relevant to the current project.
What is the process that the team is currently involved?
   A. Quality planning
   B. Quality control
   C. Quality assurance
   D. Benchmark creation

11. The change control board of your organization has approved changes that were 11.
submitted and the project team is executing them.
What would this process be considered?
   A. Executing the change request
   B. Implementing a corrective action
   C. Gold-plating
   D. Approving the change request

12. Which is the primary technique that is carried out to ensure that a contract award 12.
is executed correctly or not?
   A. Litigation
   B. Contract negotiation
   C. Inspections
   D. Procurement audit

13. In the final stages of completing a project, you and your team are involved in creating the 13.
project report that will be presented to the stakeholders. Which of the following
information is not appropriate to be included in the final report?
   A. Recommendations from your team
   B. Project success factors
   C. WBS dictionary
   D. Details of the process improvements

14. At the completion of a project, your team has completed the lessons-learned documentation 14.
and archived in the database. Who should have access to these documents?
   A. Project team members
   B. Operations department
   C. All of the company's members
   D. Functional managers

15. You are project manager for a large project that is in the final stages of completion 15.
and you need to formally provide information on the major milestone achieved.
You are also in need of immediate feedback from the stakeholders. Which is the best
communication method to meet this requirement?
   A. E-mail
   B. Web publishing
   C. Meeting
   D. Videoconferencing

16. Which document will formally authorize a project manager to start the project? 16.
   A. Project SOW
   B. Project Charter
   C. Business Case
   D. Stakeholder Register

17. Which of the following documents would be utilized to ascertain the project's investment 17.
worthiness?
   A. Project Charter
   B. Business Case
   C. Business Need
   D. Procurement documents

18. Which of the following conflict resolution is considered as Lose-lose solution?   18._____
    A. Problem-solving   C. Compromising
    B. Forcing   D. Withdrawing

19. McGregor's Theory states that all workers fit into one of the two groups. Which of the   19._____
following theories believes that people are willing to work on their own and need less
supervision?
    A. Theory X   C. Maslow's Hierarchy
    B. Theory Y   D. Expectancy

20. The major cause for conflicts on a project are schedule, project priorities and _____.   20._____

    A. cost   C. personality
    B. resources   D. management

21. The project manager is responsible for   21._____
    A. the success of the project
    B. achieving the project objectives
    C. authorizing the project
    D. performing the project work

22. Which of the following actions correspond to reducing the consequences of future   22._____
problems?
    A. Corrective action
    B. Preventive action
    C. Defect repair
    D. Change request

23. As a project manager for a large-scale project, you are in the process of procuring   23._____
materials required for the project. Which of the following documents will you not
be responsible for?
    A. Procurement documents
    B. Procurement statements of work
    C. Source selection criteria
    D. Proposals

24. During which process group will the detailed requirements be gathered?   24._____
    A. Initiating
    B. Planning
    C. Executing
    D. Closing

25. The values that illustrate PMIs code of ethics and professional conduct are   25._____
    A. respect, honesty, responsibility and honorability
    B. honesty, cultural diversity, integrity and responsibility
    C. fairness, responsibility, honesty and respect
    D. honorability, fairness, respect and responsibility

_____

KEY (CORRECT ANSWERS)

1. A		11. A	
2. D		12. D	
3. C		13. C	
4. C		14. C	
5. D		15. D	
6. C		16. B	
7. C		17. B	
8. C		18. C	
9. C		19. B	
10. C		20. B	

21. B
22. B
23. D
24. B
25. C

EXAMINATION SECTION
TEST 1

DIRECTIONS: Each question or incomplete statement is followed by several suggested answers or completions. Select the one that BEST answers the question or completes the statement. *PRINT THE LETTER OF THE CORRECT ANSWER IN THE SPACE AT THE RIGHT.*

1. *Which one* of the following generalizations is *most likely* to be INACCURATE and lead to judgmental errors in communication?   1.____

    A. A supervisor must be able to read with understanding
    B. Misunderstanding may lead to dislike
    C. Anyone can listen to another person and understand what he means
    D. It is usually desirable to let a speaker talk until he is finished

2. Assume that, as a supervisor, you have been directed to inform your subordinates about the implementation of a new procedure which will affect their work. While communicating this information, you should do all of the following EXCEPT   2.____

    A. obtain the approval of your subordinates regarding the new procedure
    B. explain the reason for implementing the new procedure
    C. hold a staff meeting at a time convenient to most of your subordinates
    D. encourage a productive discussion of the new procedure

3. Assume that you are in charge of a section that handles requests for information on matters received from the public. One day, you observe that a clerk under your supervision is using a method to log-in requests for information that is different from the one specified by you in the past. Upon questioning the clerk, you discover that instructions changing the old procedure were delivered orally by your supervisor on a day on which you were absent from the office.   3.____
Of the following, the *most appropriate* action for you to take is to

    A. tell the clerk to revert to the old procedure at once
    B. ask your supervisor for information about the change
    C. call your staff together and tell them that no existing procedure is to be changed unless you direct that it be done
    D. write a memo to your supervisor suggesting that all future changes in procedure are to be in writing and that they be directed to you

4. At the first meeting with your staff after appointment as a supervisor, you find considerable indifference and some hostility among the participants.   4.____
Of the following, the *most appropriate* way to handle this situation is to

    A. disregard the attitudes displayed and continue to make your presentation until you have completed it
    B. discontinue your presentation but continue the meeting and attempt to find out the reasons for their attitudes
    C. warm up your audience with some good natured statements and anecdotes and then proceed with your presentation
    D. discontinue the meeting and set up personal interviews with the staff members to try to find out the reason for their attitude

111

5. In order to start the training of a new employee, it has been a standard practice to have   5.__
   him read a manual of instructions or procedures.
   This method is currently being replaced by the _____ method.

    A. audio-visual   B. conference
    C. lecture   D. programmed instruction

6. Of the following subjects, the *one* that can usually be *successfully* taught by a first-line   6.__
   supervisor who is training his subordinates is:

    A. Theory and philosophy of manage-   B. Human relations
        ment
    C. Responsibilities of a supervisor   D. Job skills

7. Assume that as a supervisor you are training a clerk who is experiencing difficulty learn-   7.__
   ing a new task.
   Which one of the following would be the LEAST effective approach to take when trying
   to solve this problem? To

    A. ask questions which will reveal the clerk's understanding of the task
    B. take a different approach in explaining the task
    C. give the clerk an opportunity to ask questions about the task
    D. make sure the clerk knows you are watching his work closely

8. One school of management and supervision involves participation by employees in the   8.__
   setting of group goals and in the sharing of responsibility for the operation of the unit.
   If this philosophy were applied to a unit consisting of professional and clerical personnel, one should expect

    A. the professional and clerical personnel to participate with equal effectiveness in
        operating areas and policy areas
    B. the professional personnel to participate with greater effectiveness than the clerical
        personnel in policy areas
    C. the clerical personnel to participate with greater effectiveness than the professional
        personnel in operating areas
    D. greater participation by clerical personnel but with less responsibility for their
        actions

9. With regard to productivity, high morale among employees *generally* indicates a   9.__

    A. history of high productivity
    B. nearly absolute positive correlation with high productivity
    C. predisposition to be productive under facilitating leadership and circumstances
    D. complacency which has little effect on productivity

10. Assume that you are going to organize the professionals and clerks under your supervi-   10.__
    sion into work groups or teams of two or three employees.
    Of the following, the step which is LEAST likely to foster the successful development of
    each group is to

    A. allow friends to work together in the group
    B. provide special help and attention to employees with no friends in their group
    C. frequently switch employees from group to group
    D. rotate jobs within the group in order to strengthen group identification

11. Following are four statements which might be made by an employee to his supervisor   11.____
    during a performance evaluation interview.
    Which of the statements BEST provides a basis for developing a plan to improve the
    employee's performance?

    A. *I understand that you are dissatisfied with my work and I will try harder in the
        future.*
    B. *I feel that I've been making too many careless clerical errors recently.*
    C. *I am aware that I will be subject to disciplinary action if my work does not improve
        within one month.*
    D. *I understand that this interview is simply a requirement of your job, and not a per-
        sonal attack on me.*

12. Three months ago, Mr. Smith and his supervisor, Mrs. Jones, developed a plan which   12.____
    was intended to correct Mr. Smith's inadequate job performance. Now, during a follow-
    up interview, Mr. Smith, who thought his performance had satisfactorily improved, has
    been informed that Mrs. Jones is still dissatisfied with his work.
    Of the following, it is *most likely* that the disagreement occurred because, when formu-
    lating the plan ,they did NOT

    A. set realistic goals for Mr. Smith Is performance
    B. set a reasonable time limit for Mr. Smith to effect his improvement in performance
    C. provide for adequate training to improve Mr. Smith's skills
    D. establish performance standards for measuring Mr. Smith's progress

13. When a supervisor delegates authority to subordinates, there are usually many problems   13.____
    to overcome, such as inadequately trained subordinates and poor planning.
    All of the following are means of increasing the effectiveness of delegation EXCEPT:

    A. Defining assignments in the light of results expected
    B. Maintaining open lines of communication
    C. Establishing tight controls so that subordinates will stay within the bounds of the
        area of delegation
    D. Providing rewards for successful assumption of authority by a subordinate

14. Assume that one of your subordinates has arrived late for work several times during the   14.____
    current month. The last time he was late you had warned him that another unexcused
    lateness would result in formal disciplinary action.
    If the employee arrives late for work again during this month, the FIRST action you
    should take is to

    A. give the employee a chance to explain this lateness
    B. give the employee a written copy of your warning
    C. tell the employee that you are recommending formal disciplinary action
    D. tell the employee that you will give him only one more chance before recommend-
        ing formal disciplinary action

15. In trying to decide how many subordinates a manager can control directly, one of the determinants is how much the manager can reduce the frequency and time consumed in contacts with his subordinates.
    Of the following, the factor which LEAST influences the number and direction of these contacts is:

    A. How well the manager delegates authority
    B. The rate at which the organization is changing
    C. The control techniques used by the manager
    D. Whether the activity is line or staff

15.__

16. Systematic rotation of employees through lateral transfer within a government organization to provide for managerial development is

    A. *good,* because systematic rotation develops specialists who learn to do many jobs well
    B. *bad,* because the outsider upsets the status quo of the existing organization
    C. *good,* because rotation provides challenge and organizational flexibility
    D. *bad,* because it is upsetting to employees to be transferred within a service

16.__

17. Assume that you are required to provide an evaluation of the performance of your subordinates.
    Of the following factors, it is MOST important that the performance evaluation include a rating of each employees

    A. initiative   B. productivity   C. intelligence   D. personality

17.__

18. When preparing performance evaluations of your subordinates, *one* way to help assure that you are rating each employee fairly is to

    A. prepare a list of all employees and all the rating factors and rate all employees on one rating factor before going on to the next factor
    B. prepare a list of all your employees and all the rating factors and rate each employee on all factors before going on to the next employee
    C. discuss all the ratings you anticipate giving with another supervisor in order to obtain an unbiased opinion
    D. discuss each employee with his co-workers in order to obtain peer judgment of worth before doing any rating

18.__

19. A managerial plan which would include the GREATEST control is a plan which is

    A. spontaneous and geared to each new job that is received
    B. detailed and covering an extended time period
    C. long-range and generalized, allowing for various interpretations
    D. specific and prepared daily

19.__

20. Assume that you are preparing a report which includes statistical data covering
increases in budget allocations of four agencies for the past ten years.
For you to represent the statistical data pictorially or graphically within the report is a

20.____

    A. *poor idea,* because you should be able to make statistical data understandable
through the use of words
    B. *good idea,* because it is easier for the reader to understand pictorial representation
rather than quantities of words conveying statistical data
    C. *poor idea,* because using pictorial representation in a report may make the report
too expensive to print
    D. *good idea,* because a pictorial representation makes the report appear more
attractive than the use of many words to convey the statistical data

_____

KEY (CORRECT ANSWERS)

1.	C	11.	A
2.	A	12.	B
3.	B	13.	C
4.	D	14.	A
5.	D	15.	D
6.	D	16.	C
7.	D	17.	B
8.	B	18.	A
9.	C	19.	B
10.	C	20.	B

_____

TEST 2

DIRECTIONS: Each question or incomplete statement is followed by several suggested answers or completions. Select the one that BEST answers the question or completes the statement. *PRINT THE LETTER OF THE CORRECT ANSWER IN THE SPACE AT THE RIGHT.*

1. Research studies have shown that supervisors of groups with high production records USUALLY

    1.__

    A. give detailed instructions, constantly check on progress, and insist on approval of all decisions before implementation
    B. do considerable paperwork and other work similar to that performed by subordinates
    C. think of themselves as team members on the same level as others in the work group
    D. perform tasks traditionally associated with managerial functions

2. Mr. Smith, a bureau chief, is summoned by his agency's head in a conference to discuss Mr. Jones, an accountant who works in one of the divisions of his bureau. Mr. Jones has committed an error of such magnitude as to arouse the agency head's concern.
After agreeing with the other conferees that a severe reprimand would be the appropriate punishment, Mr. Smith should

    2.__

    A. arrange for Mr. Jones to explain the reasons for his error to the agency head
    B. send a memorandum to Mr. Jones, being careful that the language emphasizes the nature of the error rather than Mr. Jones' personal faults
    C. inform Mr. Jones' immediate supervisor of the conclusion reached at the conference, and let the supervisor take the necessary action
    D. suggest to the agency head that no additional action be taken against Mr. Jones because no further damage will be caused by the error

3. Assume that Ms. Thomson, a unit chief, has determined that the findings of an internal audit have been seriously distorted as a result of careless errors. The audit had been performed by a group of auditors in her unit and the errors were overlooked by the associate accountant in charge of the audit. Ms. Thomson has decided to delay discussing the matter with the associate accountant and the staff who performed the audit until she verifies certain details, which may require prolonged investigation.
Ms. Thomson's method of handling this situation is

    3.__

    A. *appropriate;* employees should not be accused of wrongdoing until all the facts have been determined
    B. *inappropriate;* the employees involved may assume that the errors were considered unimportant
    C. *appropriate;* employees are more likely to change their behavior as a result of disciplinary action taken after a *cooling off* period
    D. *inappropriate;* the employees involved may have forgotten the details and become emotionally upset when confronted with the facts

4. After studying the financial situation in his agency, an administrative accountant decides to recommend centralization of certain accounting functions which are being performed in three different bureaus of the organization.
The one of the following which is *most likely* to be a DISADVANTAGE if this recommendation is implemented is that

    4.____

  A. there may be less coordination of the accounting procedure because central direction is not so close to the day-to-day problems as the personnel handling them in each specialized accounting unit
  B. the higher management levels would not be able to make emergency decisions in as timely a manner as the more involved, lower-level administrators who are closer to the problem
  C. it is more difficult to focus the attention of the top management in order to resolve accounting problems because of the many other activities top management is involved in at the same time
  D. the accuracy of upward and inter-unit communication may be reduced because centralization may require insertion of more levels of administration in the chain of command

5. Of the following assumptions about the role of conflict in an organization, the *one* which is the MOST accurate statement of the approach of modern management theorists is that conflict

    5.____

  A. can usually be avoided or controlled
  B. serves as a vital element in organizational change
  C. works against attainment of organizational goals
  D. provides a constructive outlet for problem employees

6. Which of the following is generally regarded as the BEST approach for a supervisor to follow in handling grievances brought by subordinates?

    6.____

  A. Avoid becoming involved personally
  B. Involve the union representative in the first stage of discussion
  C. Settle the grievance as soon as possible
  D. Arrange for arbitration by a third party

7. Assume that supervisors of similar-sized accounting units in city, state, and federal offices were interviewed and observed at their work. It was found that the ways they acted in and viewed their roles tended to be very similar, regardless of who employed them.
Which of the following is the BEST explanation of this similarity?

    7.____

  A. A supervisor will ordinarily behave in conformance to his own self-image
  B. Each role in an organization, including the supervisory role, calls for a distinct type of personality
  C. The supervisory role reflects an exceptionally complex pattern of human response
  D. The general nature of the duties and responsibilities of the supervisory position determines the role

8. Which of the following is NOT consistent with the findings of recent research about the characteristics of successful top managers?

    A. They are *inner-directed* and not overly concerned with pleasing others
    B. They are challenged by situations filled with high risk and ambiguity
    C. They tend to stay on the same job for long periods of time
    D. They consider it more important to handle critical assignments successfully than to do routine work well

8.__

9. As a supervisor you have to give subordinate operational guidelines.
Of the following, the BEST reason for providing them with information about the overall objectives within which their operations fit is that the subordinates will

    A. be more likely to carry out the operation according to your expectations
    B. know that there is a legitimate reason for carrying out the operation in the way you have prescribed
    C. be more likely to handle unanticipated problems that may arise without having to take up your time
    D. more likely to transmit the operating instructions correctly to their subordinates

9.__

10. A supervisor holds frequent meetings with his staff.
Of the following, the BEST approach he can take in order to elicit productive discussions at these meetings is for him to

    A. ask questions of those who attend
    B. include several levels of supervisors at the meetings
    C. hold the meetings at a specified time each week
    D. begin each meeting with a statement that discussion is welcomed

10.__

11. Of the following, the MOST important action that a supervisor can take to increase the productivity of a subordinate is to

    A. increase his uninterrupted work time
    B. increase the number of reproducing machines available in the office
    C. provide clerical assistance whenever he requests it
    D. reduce the number of his assigned tasks

11.__

12. Assume that, as a supervisor, you find that you often must countermand or modify your original staff memos. If this practice continues, *which one* of the following situations is MOST likely to occur? The

    A. staff will not bother to read your memos   B. office files will become cluttered
    C. staff will delay acting on your memos   D. memos will be treated routinely

12.__

13. In making management decisions the committee approach is often used by managers.
Of the following, the BEST reason for using this approach is to

    A. prevent any one individual from assuming too much authority
    B. allow the manager to bring a wider range of experience and judgment to bear on the problem
    C. allow the participation of all staff members, which will make them feel more committed to the decisions reached
    D. permit the rapid transmission of information about decisions reached to the staff members concerned

13.__

14. In establishing standards for the measurement of the performance of a management project team, it is MOST important for the project manager to

    A. identify and define the objectives of the project
    B. determine the number of people who will be assigned to the project team
    C. evaluate the skills of the staff who will be assigned to the project team
    D. estimate fairly accurately the length of time required to complete each phase of the project

14.____

15. It is virtually impossible to tell an employee either that he is not so good as another employee or that he does not measure up to a desirable level of performance, without having him feel threatened, rejected, and discouraged.
In accordance with the foregoing observation, a supervisor who is concerned about the performance of the less efficient members of his staff should realize that

    A. he might obtain better results by not discussing the quality and quantity of their work with them, but by relying instead on the written evaluation of their performance to motivate their improvement
    B. since he is required to discuss their performance with them, he should do so in words of encouragement and in so friendly a manner as to not destroy their morale
    C. he might discuss their work in a general way, without mentioning any of the specifics about the quality of their performance, with the expectation that they would understand the full implications of his talk
    D. he should make it a point, while telling them of their poor performance, to mention that their work is as good as that of some of the other employees in the unit

15.____

16. Some advocates of management-by-objectives procedures in public agencies have been urging that this method of operations be expanded to encompass all agencies of the government, for one or more of the following reasons, not all of which may be correct:

    I. The MBO method is likely to succeed because it embraces the practice of setting near-term goals for the subordinate manager, reviewing accomplishments at an appropriate time, and repeating this process indefinitely
    II. Provision for authority to perform the tasks assigned as goals in the MBO method is normally not needed because targets are set in quantitative or qualitative terms and specific times for accomplishment are arranged in short-term, repetitive intervals
    III. Many other appraisal-of-performance programs failed because both supervisors and subordinates resisted them, while the MBO approach is not instituted until there is an organizational commitment to it
    IV. Personal accountability is clearly established through the MBO approach because verifiable results are set up in the process of formulating the targets

Which of the choices below includes ALL of the foregoing statements that are CORRECT?

    A. I and III
    C. I,II,III,IV
                           B. II and IV
                           D. I,III,IV

16.____

17. In preparing an organizational structure, the PRINCIPAL guideline for locating staff units is to place them

    A. all under a common supervisor
    B. as close as possible to the activities they serve
    C. as close to the chief executive as possible without over-extending his span of control
    D. at the lowest operational level

17.__

18. The relative importance of any unit in a department can be LEAST reliably judged by the

    A. amount of office space allocated to the unit
    B. number of employees in the unit
    C. rank of the individual who heads the unit
    D. rank of the individual to whom the unit head reports directly

18.__

19. Those who favor Planning-Programming-Budgeting Systems (PPBS) as a new method of governmental financial administration emphasize that PPBS

    A. applies statistical measurements which correlate highly with criteria
    B. makes possible economic systems analysis, including an explicit examination of alternatives
    C. makes available scarce government resources which can be coordinated on a government-wide basis and shared between local units of government
    D. shifts the emphasis in budgeting methods to an automated system of data processing

19.__

20. The term applied to computer processing which processes data concurrently with a given activity and provides results soon enough to influence the selection of a course of action is

    A. realtime processing
    B. batch processing
    C. random access processing
    D. integrated data processing

20.__

KEY (CORRECT ANSWERS)

1.	D	11.	A
2.	C	12.	C
3.	B	13.	B
4.	D	14.	A
5.	B	15.	B
6.	C	16.	D
7.	D	17.	B
8.	C	18.	B
9.	C	19.	B
10.	A	20.	A

EXAMINATION SECTION
TEST 1

DIRECTIONS: Each question or incomplete statement is followed by several suggested answers or completions. Select the one that BEST answers the question or completes the statement. *PRINT THE LETTER OF THE CORRECT ANSWER IN THE SPACE AT THE RIGHT.*

1. A management approach widely used today is based on the belief that decisions should be made and actions should be taken by managers closest to the organization's problems.
   This style of management is MOST appropriately called _____ management.

   A. scientific
   B. means-end
   C. decentralized
   D. internal process

   1.____

2. As contrasted with tall organization structures with narrow spans of control, flat organization structures with wide spans of control MOST usually provide

   A. fast communication and information flows
   B. more levels in the organizational hierarchy
   C. fewer workers reporting to supervisors
   D. lower motivation because of tighter control standards

   2.____

3. Use of the systems approach is MOST likely to lead to

   A. consideration of the impact on the whole organization of actions taken in any part of that organization
   B. the placing of restrictions on departmental authority
   C. use of mathematical models to suboptimize production
   D. consideration of the activities of each unit of an organization as a totality without regard to the remainder of the organization

   3.____

4. An administrator, with overall responsibility for all administrative operations in a large operating agency, is considering organizing the agency's personnel office around either of the following two alternative concepts:
   Alternative I-   a corps of specialists for each branch of personnel subject matter, whose skills, counsel, or work products are coordinated only by the agency personnel officer
   Alternative II-   a crew of so-called *personnel generalists,* who individually work with particular segments of the organization but deal with all subspecial-ties of the personnel function
   The one of the following which MOST tends to be a DRAWBACK of Alternative I, as compared with Alternative II, is that

   A. training and employee relations work call for education, interests, and talents that differ from those required for classification and compensation work
   B. personnel office staff may develop only superficial familiarity with the specialized areas to which they have been assigned
   C. supervisors may fail to get continuing overall personnel advice on an integrated basis
   D. the personnel specialists are likely to become so interested in and identified with the operating view as to particular cases that they lose their professional objectivity and become merely advocates of what some supervisor wants

   4.____

5. The matrix summary or decision matrix is a useful tool for making choices. Its effectiveness is MOST dependent upon the user's ability to   5.___

    A. write a computer program (Fortran or Cobol)
    B. assign weights representing the relative importance of the objectives
    C. solve a set of two equations with two unknowns
    D. work with matrix algebra

6. An organizational form which is set up only on an *ad hoc* basis to meet specific goals is said PRIMARILY to use   6.___

    A. clean break departmentation
    B. matrix or task force organization
    C. scalar specialization
    D. geographic or area-wide decentralization

7. The concept of job enlargement would LEAST properly be implemented by   7.___

    A. permitting workers to follow through on tasks or projects from start to finish
    B. delegating the maximum authority possible for decision-making to lower levels in the hierarchy
    C. maximizing the number of professional classes in the classification plan
    D. training employees to grow beyond whatever tasks they have been performing

8. As used in the area of administration, the principle of *unity of command* MOST specifically means that   8.___

    A. an individual should report to only one superior for any single activity
    B. individuals make better decisions than do committees
    C. in large organizations, chains of command are normally too long
    D. an individual should not supervise over five subordinates

9. The methods of operations research, statistical decision-making, and linear programming have been referred to as the tool kit of the manager.
Utilization of these tools is LEAST useful in the performance of which of the following functions?   9.___

    A. Elimination of the need for using judgment when making decisions
    B. Facilitation of decision-making without the need for sub-optimization
    C. Quantifying problems for management study
    D. Research and analysis of management operations

10. When acting in their respective managerial capacities, the chief executive officer and the office supervisor both perform the fundamental functions of management. Of the following differences between the two, the one which is generally considered to be the LEAST significant is the   10.___

    A. breadth of the objectives
    B. complexity of measuring actual efficiency of performance
    C. number of decisions made
    D. organizational relationships affected by actions taken

11. The ability of operations researchers to solve complicated problems rests on their use of models.   11.____
    These models can BEST be described as

    A. mathematical statements of the problem
    B. physical constructs that simulate a work layout
    C. toy-like representations of employees in work environments
    D. role-playing simulations

12. Of the following, it is MOST likely to be proper for the agency head to allow the agency personnel officer to make final selection of appointees from certified eligible lists where there are   12.____

    A. *small* numbers of employees to be hired in newly-developed professional fields
    B. *large* numbers of persons to be hired for key managerial positions
    C. *large* numbers of persons to be hired in very routine occupations where the individual discretion of operating officials is not vital
    D. *small* numbers of persons to be hired in highly specialized professional occupations which are vital to the agency's operations

13. Of the following, an operating agency personnel office is LEAST likely to be able to exert strong influence or control within the operating agency by   13.____

    A. interpreting to the operating agency head what is intended by the directives and rules emanating from the central personnel agency
    B. establishing the key objectives of those line divisions of the operating agency employing large numbers of staff and operating under the management-by-objectives approach
    C. formulating and proposing to the agency head the internal policies and procedures on personnel matters required within the operating agency
    D. exercising certain discretionary authority in the application of the agency head's general personnel policies to actual specific situations

14. PERT is a recently developed system used *primarily* to   14.____

    A. evaluate the quality of applicants' backgrounds
    B. analyze and control the timing aspects of a major project
    C. control the total expenditure of agency funds within a monthly or quarterly time period
    D. analyze and control the differential effect on costs of purchasing in different quantities

15. Assume that an operating agency has among its vacant positions two positions, each of which encompasses mixed duties. Both require appointees to have considerable education and experience, but these requirements are essential only for the more difficult duties of these positions. In the place of these positions, an administrator creates two new positions, one in which the higher duties are concentrated and the other with the lesser functions requiring only minimum preparation.   15.____
    Of the following, it is generally MOST appropriate to characterize the administrator's action as a(n)

A.   *undesirable* example of deliberate downgrading of standards and requirements
B.   *undesirable* manipulation of the classification system for non-merit purposes
C.   *desirable* broadening of the definition of a class of positions
D.   *desirable* example of job redesign

16.   Of the following, the LEAST important stumbling block to the development of personnel   16.__
mobility among governmental jurisdictions is the

A.   limitations on lateral entry above junior levels in many jurisdictions
B.   continued collection of filing fees for civil service tests by many governmental juris-
dictions
C.   absence of reciprocal exchange of retirement benefit eligibility between govern-
ments
D.   disparities in salary scales between governments

17.   Of the following, the MAJOR disadvantage of a personnel system that features the *selec-*   17.__
tion out (forced retirement) of those who have been passed over a number of times for
promotion is that such a system

A.   wastes manpower which is perfectly competent at one level but unable to rise
above that level
B.   wastes funds by requiring review boards
C.   leads to excessive recruiting of newcomers from outside the system
D.   may not be utilized in *closed* career systems with low maximum age limits for
entrance

18.   Of the following, the fields in which operating agency personnel offices generally exercise   18.__
the MOST stringent controls over first line supervisors in the agency are

A.   methods analysis and work simplification
B.   selection and position classification
C.   vestibule training and Gantt chart
D.   suggestion systems and staff development

19.   Of the following, computers are normally MOST effective in handling   19.__

A.   large masses of data requiring simple processing
B.   small amounts of data requiring constantly changing complex processing
C.   data for which reported values are often subject to inaccuracies
D.   large amounts of data requiring continual programming and reprocessing

20.   Contingency planning, which has long been used by the military and is assuming   20.__
increasing importance in other organizations, may BEST be described as a process
which utilizes

A.   alternative plans based on varying assumptions
B.   *crash programs* by organizations departmentalized along process lines
C.   plans which mandate substitution of equipment for manpower at predetermined
operational levels
D.   plans that individually and accurately predict future events

21. In the management of inventory, two kinds of costs normally determine when to order   21.____
    and in what amounts. The one of the following choices which includes BOTH of these
    kinds of costs is _____ costs and _____ costs.

    A. carrying; storage   B. personnel; order
    C. computer; order   D. personnel; computer

22. At top management levels, the one of the following which is generally the MOST impor-   22.____
    tant executive skill is skill in

    A. budgeting procedures
    B. a technical discipline
    C. controlling actions in accordance with previously approved plans
    D. seeing the organization as a whole

23. Of the following, the BEST way to facilitate the successful operation of a committee is to   23.____
    set guidelines establishing its

    A. budget exclusive of personnel costs
    B. location
    C. schedule of meetings or conferences
    D. scope or purpose

24. Executive training programs that single out particular managers and groom them for pro-   24.____
    motion create the so-called organizational *crown princes.*
    Of the following, the MOST serious problem that arises in connection with this
    practice is that

    A. the managers chosen for promotion seldom turn out to be the best managers
       since the future potential of persons cannot be predicted
    B. not enough effort is made to remove organizational obstacles in the way of their
       development and achievement
    C. the resentment of the managers not selected for the program has an adverse
       effect on the motivation of those managers not selected
    D. performance appraisal and review are not carried out systematically enough

25. Of the following, the LEAST likely result of the use of the concept of job enlargement is   25.____
    that

    A. coordination will be simplified
    B. the individual's job will become less challenging
    C. worker satisfaction will increase
    D. fewer people will have to give attention to each piece of work

KEY (CORRECT ANSWERS)

1.	C		11.	A
2.	A		12.	C
3.	A		13.	B
4.	C		14.	B
5.	B		15.	D
6.	B		16.	B
7.	C		17.	A
8.	A		18.	B
9.	A		19.	A
10.	C		20.	A

21.	A
22.	D
23.	D
24.	C
25.	B

TEST 2

DIRECTIONS: Each question or incomplete statement is followed by several suggested answers or completions. Select the one that BEST answers the question or completes the statement. *PRINT THE LETTER OF THE CORRECT ANSWER IN THE SPACE AT THE RIGHT.*

1. The one of the following which is MOST likely to be emphasized in the use of the brain-storming technique is the

    A. early consideration of cost factors of all ideas which may be suggested
    B. avoidance of impractical suggestions
    C. separation of the generation of ideas from their evaluation
    D. appraisal of suggestions concurrently with their initial presentation

1.____

2. Of the following, the BEST method for assessing managerial performance is generally to

    A. compare the manager's accomplishments against clear, specific, agreed-upon goals
    B. compare the manager's traits with those of his peers on a predetermined objective scale
    C. measure the manager's behavior against a listing of itemized personal traits
    D. measure the manager's success according to the enumeration of the *satisfaction* principle

2.____

3. As compared with recruitment from outside, selection from within the service must generally show GREATER concern for the

    A. prestige in which the public service as a whole is held by the public
    B. morale of the candidate group comprising the recruitment field
    C. cost of examining per candidate
    D. benefits of the use of standardized and validated tests

3.____

4. Performance budgeting focuses PRIMARY attention upon which one of the following? The

    A. things to be acquired, such as supplies and equipment
    B. general character and relative importance of the work to be done or the service to be rendered
    C. list of personnel to be employed, by specific title
    D. separation of employee performance evaluations from employee compensation

4.____

5. Of the following, the FIRST step in the installation and operation of a performance budgeting system generally should be the

    A. identification of program costs in relationship to the accounting system and operating structure
    B. identification of the specific end results of past programs in other jurisdictions
    C. identification of work programs that are meaningful for management purposes
    D. establishment of organizational structures each containing only one work program

5.____

6. Of the following, the MOST important purpose of a system of quarterly allotments of appropriated funds generally is to enable the

   6.__

   A. head of the judicial branch to determine the legality of agency requests for budget increases
   B. operating agencies of government to upgrade the quality of their services without increasing costs
   C. head of the executive branch to control the rate at which the operating agencies obligate and expend funds
   D. operating agencies of government to avoid payment for services which have not been properly rendered by employees

7. In the preparation of the agency's budget, the agency's central budget office has two responsibilities: program review and management improvement.
   Which one of the following questions concerning an operating agency's program is MOST closely related to the agency budget officer's program review responsibility?

   7.__

   A. Can expenditures for supplies, materials, or equipment be reduced?
   B. Will improved work methods contribute to a more effective program?
   C. What is the relative importance of this program as compared with other programs?
   D. Will a realignment of responsibilities contribute to a higher level of program performance?

8. Of the following, the method of evaluating relative rates of return normally and generally thought to be MOST useful in evaluating government operations is _____ analysis.

   8.__

   A. cost-benefit
   C. investment capital
   B. budget variance
   D. budget planning program

9. The one of the following assumptions that is LEAST likely to be made by a democratic or permissive type of leader is that

   9.__

   A. commitment to goals is seldom a result of monetary rewards alone
   B. people can learn not only to accept, but also to seek, responsibility
   C. the average person prefers security over advancement
   D. creativity may be found in most segments of the population

10. In attempting to motivate subordinates, a manager should PRINCIPALLY be aware of the fact that

   10.__

   A. the psychological qualities of people, in general, are easily predictable
   B. fear, as a traditional form of motivation, has lost much of its former power to motivate people in our modern industrial society
   C. fear is still the most potent force in motivating the behavior of subordinates in the public service
   D. the worker has very little control over the quality and quantity of his output

11. Assume that the following figures represent the number of work-units that were produced during a week by each of sixteen employees in a division:

              12   16   13   18
              21   12   16   13
              16   13   17   21
              13   15   18   20

If all of the employees of the division who produced thirteen work-units during the week had instead produced fifteen work-units during that same week, then for that week, the

   A. mean, median, and mode would all change
   B. mean and mode would change, but the median would remain the same
   C. mode and median would change, but the mean would remain the same
   D. mode, mean, and median would all still remain unchanged in value

11.____

12. An important law in motivation theory is called the *law of effect.* This law says that behavior which satisfies a person's needs tends to be repeated; behavior which does not satisfy a person's needs tends to be eliminated. The one of the following which is the BEST interpretation of this law is that

   A. productivity depends on personality traits
   B. diversity of goals leads to instability of motivation
   C. the greater the satisfaction, the more likely it is that the behavior will be reinforced
   D. extrinsic satisfaction is more important than intrinsic reward

12.____

13. Of the following, the MOST acceptable reason an administrator can give for taking advice from other employees in the organization only when he asks for it is that he wants to

   A. encourage creativity and high morale
   B. keep dysfunctional pressures and inconsistent recommendations to a minimum
   C. show his superiors and peers who is in charge
   D. show his subordinates who is in charge

13.____

14. A complete picture of the communication channels in an organization can BEST be revealed by

   A. observing the planned paperwork system
   B. recording the highly intermittent patterns of communication
   C. plotting the entire flow of information over a period of time
   D. monitoring the *grapevine*

14.____

Questions 15-16.

DIRECTIONS: Answer Questions 15 and 16 SOLELY on the basis of the passage below.

Management by objectives (MBO) may be defined as the process by which the superior and the subordinate managers of an organization jointly define its common goals, define each individual's major areas of responsibility in terms of the results expected of him and use these measures as guides for operating the unit and assessing the contribution of each of its members.

The MBO approach requires that after organizational goals are established and communicated, targets must be set for each individual position which are congruent with organizational goals. Periodic performance reviews and a final review using the objectives set as criteria are also basic to this approach.

Recent studies have shown that MBO programs are influenced by attitudes and perceptions of the boss, the company, the reward-punishment system, and the program itself. In addition, the manner in which the MBO program is carried out can influence the success of the program. A study done in the late sixties indicates that the best results are obtained when the manager sets goals which deal with significant problem areas in the organizational unit, or with the subordinate's personal deficiencies. These goals must be clear with regard to what is expected of the subordinate. The frequency of feedback is also important in the success of a management-by-Objectives program. Generally, the greater the amount of feedback, the more successful the MBO program.

15. According to the above passage, the expected output for individual employees should be determined   15.__

    A. after a number of reviews of work performance
    B. after common organizational goals are defined
    C. before common organizational goals are defined
    D. on the basis of an employee's personal qualities

16. According to the above passage, the management-by-objectives approach requires   16.__

    A. less feedback than other types of management programs
    B. little review of on-the-job performance after the initial setting of goals
    C. general conformance between individual goals and organizational goals
    D. the setting of goals which deal with minor problem areas in the organization

Questions 17-19.

DIRECTIONS: Answer Questions 17 to 19 SOLELY on the basis of the passage below.

During the last decade, a great deal of interest has been generated around the phenomenon of organizational development, or the process of developing human resources through conscious organisation effort. Organizational development (OD) stresses improving interpersonal relationships and organizational skills, such as communication, to a much greater degree than individual training ever did.

The kind of training that an organization should emphasize depends upon the present and future structure of the organization. If future organizations are to be unstable, shifting coalitions, then individual skills and abilities, particularly those emphasizing innovativeness, creativity, flexibility, and the latest technological knowledge, are crucial, and individual training is most appropriate.

But if there is to be little change in organizational structure, then the main thrust of training should be group-oriented or organizational development. This approach seems better designed for overcoming hierarchical barriers, for developing a degree of interpersonal relationships which make communication along the chain of command possible, and for retaining a modicum of innovation and/or flexibility.

17. According to the above passage, group-oriented training is MOST useful in   17.____

    A. developing a communications system that will facilitate understanding through the chain of command
    B. highly flexible and mobile organizations
    C. preventing the crossing of hierarchical barriers within an organization
    D. saving energy otherwise wasted on developing methods of dealing with rigid hierarchies

18. The one of the following conclusions which can be drawn MOST appropriately from the   18.____
above passage is that

    A. behavioral research supports the use of organizational development training methods rather than individualized training
    B. it is easier to provide individualized training in specific skills than to set up sensitivity training programs
    C. organizational development eliminates innovative or flexible activity
    D. the nature of an organization greatly influences which training methods will be most effective

19. According to the above passage, the one of the following which is LEAST important for   19.____
large-scale organizations geared to rapid and abrupt change is

    A. current technological information
    B. development of a high degree of interpersonal relationships
    C. development of individual skills and abilities
    D. emphasis on creativity

Questions 20-25.

DIRECTIONS: Each of Questions 20 through 25 consists of a statement which contains one word that is incorrectly used because it is not in keeping with the meaning that the quotation is evidently intended to convey. Determine which word is INCORRECTLY used. Select from the choices lettered A, B, C, and D the word which, when substituted for the incorrectly used word, would BEST help to convey the meaning of the statement.

20. One of the considerations likely to affect the currency of classification, particularly in professional and managerial occupations, is the impact of the incumbent's capacities on the job. Some work is highly susceptible to change as the result of the special talents or interests of the classifier. Organization should never be so rigid as not to capitalize on the innovative or unusual proclivities of its key employees. While a machine operator may not be able, even subtly, to change the character or level of his job, the design engineer, the attorney, or the organization and methods analyst might readily do so. Reliance on his judgment and the scope of his assignments may both grow as the result of his skill, insight, and capacity.   20.__

   A. unlikely   B. incumbent   C. directly   D. scope

21. The supply of services by the state is not governed by market price. The aim is to supply such services to all who need them and to treat all consumers equally. This objective especially compels the civil servant to maintain a role of strict impartiality, based on the principle of equality of individual citizens vis-a-vis their government. However, there is a clear difference between being neutral and being impartial. If the requirement is construed to mean that all civil servants should be political eunuchs, devoid of the drive and motivation essential to dynamic administration, then the concept of impartiality is being seriously utilized. Modern governments should not be stopped from demanding that their hirelings have not only the technical but the emotional qualifications necessary for whole-hearted effort.   21.__

   A. determined   B. rule   C. stable   D. misapplied

22. The manager was barely listening. Recently, at the divisional level, several new fronts of troubles had erupted, including a requirement to increase production yet hold down operating costs and somehow raise quality standards. Though the three objectives were basically obsolete, top departmental management was insisting on the simultaneous attainment of them, an insistence not helping the manager's ulcer, an old enemy within. Thus, the manager could not find time for interest in individuals-only in statistics which regiments of individuals, like unconsidered Army privates, added up to.   22.__

   A. quantity   B. battalion   C. incompatible   D. quiet

23. When a large volume of data flows directly between operators and first-line supervisors, senior executives tend to be out of the mainstream of work. Summary reports can increase their remoteness. An executive needs to know the volume, quality, and cost of completed work, and exceptional problems. In addition, he may desire information on key operating conditions. Summary reports on these matters are, therefore, essential features of a communications network and make delegation without loss of control possible.   23.__

   A. unimportant   B. quantity
   C. offset   D. incomplete

24. Of major significance in management is harmony between the overall objectives of the organization and the managerial objectives within that organization. In addition, harmony among goals of managers is impossible; they should not be at cross-purposes. Each manager's goal should supplement and assist the goals of his colleagues. Likewise, the objectives of individuals or nonmanagement members should be harmonized with those of the manager. When this is accomplished, genuine teamwork is the result, and human relations are aided materially. The integration of managers' and individuals' goals aids in achieving greater work satisfaction at all levels.

24.____

   A. competition   B. dominate
   C. incremental   D. vital

25. Change constantly challenges the manager. Some of this change is evolutionary, some revolutionary, some recognizable, some nonrecognizable. Both forces within an enterprise and forces outside the enterprise cause managers to act and react in initiating changes in their immediate working environment. Change invalidates existing operations. Goals are not being accomplished in the best manner, problems develop, and frequently because of the lack of time, only patched-up solutions are followed. The result is that the mode of management is profound in nature and temporary in effectiveness. A complete overhaul of managerial operations should take place. It appears quite likely that we are just beginning to see the real effects of change in our society; the pace probably will accelerate in ways that few really understand or know how to handle.

25.____

   A. confirms   B. decline
   C. instituting   D. superficial

KEY (CORRECT ANSWERS)

1.	C		11.	B
2.	A		12.	C
3.	B		13.	B
4.	B		14.	C
5.	C		15.	B
6.	C		16.	C
7.	C		17.	A
8.	A		18.	D
9.	C		19.	B
10.	B		20.	B

21.	D
22.	C
23.	C
24.	D
25.	D

EXAMINATION SECTION
TEST 1

DIRECTIONS: Each question or incomplete statement is followed by several suggested answers or completions. Select the one that BEST answers the question or completes the statement. *PRINT THE LETTER OF THE CORRECT ANSWER IN THE SPACE AT THE RIGHT.*

1. Assume that a manager is preparing a list of reasons to justify making a major change in methods and procedures in his agency.
Which of the following reasons would be LEAST appropriate on such a list?

    A. Improve the means for satisfying needs and wants of agency personnel
    B. Increase efficiency
    C. Intensify competition and stimulate loyalty to separate work groups
    D. Contribute to the individual and group satisfaction of agency personnel

1.____

2. Many managers recognize the benefits of decentralization but are concerned about the danger of over-relaxation of control as a result of increased delegation.
Of the following, the MOST appropriate means of establishing proper control under decentralization is for the manager to

    A. establish detailed standards for all phases of operation
    B. shift his attention from operating details to appraisal of results
    C. keep himself informed by decreasing the time span covered by reports
    D. make unilateral decisions on difficult situations that arise in decentralized locations

2.____

3. In some agencies, the counsel to the agency head is given the right to bypass the chain of command and issue orders directly to the staff concerning matters that involve certain specific processes and practices.
This situation MOST NEARLY illustrates the principle of

    A. the acceptance theory of authority
    B. multiple-linear authority
    C. splintered authority
    D. functional authority

3.____

4. Assume that a manager is writing a brief report to his superior outlining the advantages of matrix organization. Of the following, it would be INCORRECT to state that

    A. in matrix organization, a project is emphasized by designating one individual as the focal point for all matters pertaining to it
    B. utilization of manpower can be flexible in matrix organization because a reservoir of specialists is maintained in the line operations
    C. the usual line staff arrangement is generally reversed in matrix organization
    D. in matrix organization, responsiveness to project needs is generally faster due to establishing needed communication lines and decision points

4.____

5. It is commonly understood that communication is an important part of the administrative process.
Which of the following is NOT a valid principle of the communication process in administration?

    A. The channels of communication should be spontaneous.
    B. The lines of communication should be as direct and as short as possible.
    C. Communications should be authenticated.
    D. The persons serving in communications centers should be competent.

    5._

6. The PRIMARY purpose of the quantitative approach in management is to

    A. identify better alternatives for management decision-making
    B. substitute data for judgment
    C. match opinions to data
    D. match data to opinions

    6._

7. If an executive wants to make a strong case for running his agency as a flat type of structure, he should point out that the PRIMARY advantage of doing so is to

    A. provide less experience in decision-making for agency personnel
    B. facilitate frequent contact between each superior and his immediate subordinates
    C. improve communication and unify attitudes
    D. improve communication and diversify attitudes

    7._

8. In deciding how detailed his delegation of authority to a subordinate should be, a manager should follow the general principle that

    A. delegation of authority is more detailed at the top of the organizational structure
    B. detailed delegation of authority is associated with detailed work assignments
    C. delegation of authority should be in sufficient detail to prevent overlapping assignments
    D. detailed delegation of authority is associated with broad work assignments

    8._

9. In recent years, newer and more fluid types of organizational forms have been developed. One of these is a type of free-form organization.
Another name for this type of organization is the

    A. project organization   B. semimix organization
    C. naturalistic structure   D. semipermanent structure

    9._

10. Which of the following is the MAJOR objective of operational or management systems audits?

    A. Determining the number of personnel needed
    B. Recommending opportunities for improving operating and management practices
    C. Detecting fraud
    D. Determining organization problems

    10._

11. Assume that a manager observes that conflict exists between his agency and another operating agency of government.
Which of the following statements is the LEAST probable cause of this conflict?

    A. Incompatibility between the agencies' goals but similarity in their resource allocations
    B. Compatibility between agencies' goals and resources
    C. Status differences between agency personnel
    D. Differences in perceptions of each other's policies

11.____

12. Of the following, a MAJOR purpose of brainstorming as a problem-solving technique is to

    A. develop the ability to concentrate
    B. encourage creative thinking
    C. evaluate employees' ideas
    D. develop critical ability

12.____

13. The one of the following requirements which is LEAST likely to accompany regular delegation of work from a manager to a subordinate is a(n)

    A. need to review the organization's workload
    B. indication of what work the subordinate is to do
    C. need to grant authority to the subordinate
    D. obligation for the subordinate who accepts the work to try to complete it

13.____

14. Of the following, the one factor which is generally considered LEAST essential to successful committee operation is

    A. stating a clear definition of the authority and scope of the committee
    B. selecting the committee chairman carefully
    C. limiting the size of the committee to four persons
    D. limiting the subject matter to that which can be handled in group discussion

14.____

15. In using the program evaluation and review technique, the *critical path* is the path that

    A. requires the shortest time
    B. requires the longest time
    C. focuses most attention on social constraints
    D. focuses most attention on repetitious jobs

15.____

16. Which one of the following is LEAST characteristic of the management-by-objectives approach?

    A. The scope within which the employee may exercise decision-making is broadened
    B. The employee starts with a self-appraisal of his performances, abilities, and potential
    C. Emphasis is placed on activities performed; activities orientation is maximized
    D. Each employee participates in determining his own objectives

16.____

17. The function of management which puts into effect the decisions, plans, and programs that have previously been worked out for achieving the goals of the group is MOST appropriately called

    A. scheduling   B. classifying
    C. budgeting   D. directing

17.___

18. In the establishment of a plan to improve office productive efficiency, which of the following guidelines is LEAST helpful in setting sound work standards?

    A. Employees must accept the plan's objectives.
    B. Current production averages must be promulgated as work standards for a group.
    C. The work flow must generally be fairly constant.
    D. The operation of the plan must be expressed in terms understandable to the worker.

18.___

19. The one of the following activities which, generally speaking, is of *relatively* MAJOR importance at the lower-management level and of *somewhat* LESSER importance at higher-management levels is

    A. actuating   B. forecasting
    C. organizing   D. planning

19.___

20. Three styles of leadership exist: democratic, authoritarian, and laissez-faire.
Of the following work situations, the one in which a democratic approach would normally be the MOST effective is when the work is

    A. routine and moderately complex
    B. repetitious and simple
    C. complex and not routine
    D. simple and not routine

20.___

21. Governmental and business organizations *generally* encounter the GREATEST difficulties in developing tangible measures of which one of the following?

    A. The level of expenditures
    B. Contributions to social welfare
    C. Retention rates
    D. Causes of labor unrest

21.___

22. Of the following, a *management-by-objectives* program is BEST described as

    A. a new comprehensive plan of organization
    B. introduction of budgets and financial controls
    C. introduction of long–range planning
    D. development of future goals with supporting and related progress reviews

22.___

23. Research and analysis is probably the most widely used technique for selecting alternatives when major planning decisions are involved.
Of the following, a VALUABLE characteristic of research and analysis is that this technique

    A. places the problem in a meaningful conceptual framework
    B. involves practical application of the various alternatives
    C. accurately analyzes all important tangibles
    D. is much less expensive than other problem-solving methods

23.____

24. If a manager were assigned the task of using a systems approach to designing a new work unit, which of the following should he consider FIRST in carrying out his design?

    A. Networks
    B. Work flows and information processes
    C. Linkages and relationships
    D. Decision points and control loops

24.____

25. The MAIN distinction between Theory X and Theory Y approaches to organization, in accordance with Douglas McGregor's view, is that Theory Y

    A. considers that work is natural to people; Theory X assumes that people are lazy and avoid work
    B. leads to a tall, narrow organization structure, while Theory X leads to one that is flat
    C. organizations motivate people with money; Theory X organizations motivate people with good working conditions
    D. represents authoritarian management, while Theory X management is participative

25.____

———————

KEY (CORRECT ANSWERS)

1.	C		11.	B
2.	B		12.	B
3.	D		13.	A
4.	C		14.	C
5.	A		15.	B
6.	A		16.	C
7.	C		17.	D
8.	B		18.	B
9.	A		19.	A
10.	B		20.	C

21.	B
22.	D
23.	A
24.	B
25.	A

———

TEST 2

DIRECTIONS: Each question or incomplete statement is followed by several suggested answers or completions. Select the one that BEST answers the question or completes the statement. *PRINT THE LETTER OF THE CORRECT ANSWER IN THE SPACE AT THE RIGHT.*

1. Of the following, the stage in decision-making which is usually MOST difficult is   1.____

    A. stating the alternatives
    B. predicting the possible outcome of each alternative
    C. evaluating the relative merits of each alternative
    D. minimizing the undesirable aspects of the alternative selected

2. In a department where a clerk is reporting both to a senior clerk in charge of the mail   2.____
   room and also to a supervising clerk in charge of the duplicating section, there may be a
   breakdown of the management principle called

    A. horizontal specialization   B. job enrichment
    C. unity of command   D. Graicunas' Law

3. Of the following, the failure by line managers to accept and appreciate the benefits and   3.____
   limitations of a new program or system VERY frequently can be traced to the

    A. budgetary problems involved
    B. resultant need to reduce staff
    C. lack of controls it engenders
    D. failure of top management to support its implementation

4. Although there is general agreement that *management by objectives* has made a major   4.____
   contribution to modern management of large organizations, criticisms of the system during the past few years have resulted in

    A. mounting pressure for relaxation of management goals
    B. renewed concern with human values and the manager's personal needs
    C. over-mechanistic application of the perceptions of the behavioral scientists
    D. disillusionment with *management by objectives* on the part of a majority of manag-
       ers

5. Of the following, which is usually considered to be a MAJOR obstacle to the systematic   5.____
   analysis of potential problems by managers?

    A. Managers have a tendency to think that all the implications of some proposed step
       cannot be fully understood.
    B. Rewards rarely go to those managers who are most successful at resolving current
       problems in management.
    C. There is a common conviction of managers that their goals are difficult to achieve.
    D. Managers are far more concerned about correcting today's problems than with pre-
       venting tomorrow's.

6. Which of the following should generally have the MOST influence on the selection of supervisors?

    A. Experience within the work unit where the vacancies exist
    B. Amount of money needed to effect the promotion
    C. Personal preferences of the administration
    D. Evaluation of capacity to exercise supervisory responsibilities

    6._

7. In questioning a potential administrator for selection purposes, the one of the following practices which is MOST desirable is to

    A. encourage the job applicant to give primarily *yes* or *no* replies
    B. get the applicant to talk freely and in detail about his background
    C. let the job applicant speak most of the time
    D. probe the applicant's attitudes, motivation, and willingness to accept responsibility

    7._

8. In implementing the managerial function of training subordinates, it is USEFUL to know that a widely agreed-upon definition of human learning is that learning

    A. is a relatively permanent change in behavior that results from reinforced practice or experience
    B. involves an improvement, but not necessarily a change in behavior
    C. involves a change in behavior, but not necessarily an improvement
    D. is a temporary change in behavior which must be subject to practice or experience

    8._

9. If a manager were thinking about using a committee of subordinates to solve an operating problem, which of the following would generally NOT be an advantage of such use of the committee approach?

    A. Improved coordination
    B. Low cost
    C. Increased motivation
    D. Integrated judgment

    9._

10. Which one of the following management approaches MOST often uses model-building techniques to solve management problems?
    _____ approach

    A. Behavioral
    B. Fiscal
    C. Quantitative
    D. Process

    10._

11. Of the following, the MOST serious risk in using budgets as a tool for management control is the

    A. probable neglect of other good management practices
    B. likelihood of guesswork because of the need to plan far in advance
    C. possibility of undue emphasis on factors that are easiest to measure
    D. danger of making qualitative rather than quantitative assessments of performance

    11._

12. In government budgeting, the problem of relating financial transactions to the fiscal year 12.____
in which they are budgeted is BEST met by

    A. determining the cash balance by comparing how much money has been received
and how much has been paid out
    B. applying net revenue to the fiscal year in which they are collected as offset by rele-
vant expenses
    C. adopting a system whereby appropriations are entered when they are received
and expenditures are entered when they are paid out
    D. entering expenditures on the books when the obligation to make the expenditure is
made

13. If the agency's bookkeeping system records income when it is received and expenditures 13.____
when the money is paid out, this sytem is USUALLY known as a _____ system.

    A. cash   B. flow-payment
    C. deferred   D. fiscal year income

14. An audit, as the term applies to budget execution, is MOST NEARLY a 14.____

    A. procedure based on the budget estimates
    B. control exercised by the executive on the legislature in the establishment of pro-
gram priorities
    C. check on the legality of expenditures and is based on the appropriations act
    D. requirement which must be met before funds can be spent

15. In government budgeting, there is a procedure known as *allotment*. 15.____
Of the following statements which relate to allotment, select the one that is MOST gen-
erally considered to be correct.
Allotment

    A. increases the practice of budget units coming back to the legislative branch for
supplemental appropriations
    B. is simply an example of red tape
    C. eliminates the requirement of timing of expenditures
    D. is designed to prevent waste

16. In government budgeting, the establishment of the schedules of allotments is MOST 16.____
generally the responsibility of the

    A. budget unit and the legislature
    B. budget unit and the executive
    C. budget unit *only*
    D. executive and the legislature

17. Of the following statements relating to preparation of an organization's budget request, which is the MOST generally valid precaution?   17.__

    A. Give specific instructions on the format of budget requests and required supporting data
    B. Because of the complexity of preparing a budget request, avoid argumentation to support the requests
    C. Put requests in whatever format is desirable
    D. Consider that final approval will be given to initial estimates

18. Of the following statements which relate to the budget process in a well–organized government, select the one that is MOST NEARLY correct.   18.__

    A. The budget cycle is the step-by-step process which is repeated each and every fiscal year.
    B. Securing approval of the budget does not take place within the budget cycle.
    C. The development of a new budget and putting it into effect is a two-step process known as the budget cycle.
    D. The fiscal period, usually a fiscal year, has no relation to the budget cycle.

19. If a manager were asked what PPBS stands for, he would be RIGHT if he said   19.__

    A. public planning budgeting system
    B. planning programming budgeting system
    C. planning projections budgeting system
    D. programming procedures budgeting system

Questions 20–21.

DIRECTIONS: Answer Questions 20 and 21 on the basis of the following information.

Sample Budget

Refuse Collection	Amount
Personal Services	$ 30,000
Contractual Services	5,000
Supplies and Materials	5,000
Capital Outlay	10,000
	$ 50,000

Residential Collections		
Dwellings–1 pickup per week		1,000
Tons of refuse collected per year		375
Cost of collections per ton	$	8
Cost per dwelling pickup per year	$	3
Total annual cost	$	3,000

20. The sample budget shown is a simplified example of a _____ budget.　　　　　20._____

    A.　factorial　　　　　　　　　　B.　performance
    C.　qualitative　　　　　　　　　 D.　rational

21. The budget shown in the sample differs CHIEFLY from line-item and program budgets in　21._____
that it includes

    A.　objects of expenditure but not activities or functions
    B.　only activities, functions, and control
    C.　activities and functions but not objects of expenditures
    D.　levels of service

Question 22.

DIRECTIONS:　Answer Question 22 on the basis of the following information.

Sample Budget

Environmental Safety		
Air Pollution Protection		
Personal Services	*$20,000,000*	
Contractual Services	*4,000,000*	
Supplies and Materials	*4,000,000*	
Capital Outlay	*2,000,000*	
Total Air Pollution Protection		*$ 30,000,000*
Water Pollution Protection		
Personal Services	*$23,000,000*	
Supplies and Materials	*4,500,000*	
Capital Outlay	*20,500,000*	
Total Water Pollution Protection		*$ 48,000,000*
Total Environmental Safety		*$ 78,000,000*

22. Based on the above budget, which is the MOST valid statement?　　　　　　22._____

    A.　Environmental Safety, Air Pollution Protection, and Water Pollution Protection could
       all be considered program elements.
    B.　The object listings included water pollution protection and capital outlay.
    C.　Examples of the program element listings in the above are personal services and
       supplies and materials.
    D.　Contractual Services and Environmental Safety were the program element listings.

23. Which of the following is NOT an advantage of a program budget over a line-item bud-　23._____
get?
A program budget

    A.　allows us to set up priority lists in deciding what activities we will spend our money
       on
    B.　gives us more control over expenditures than a line-item budget
    C.　is more informative in that we know the broad purposes of spending money
    D.　enables us to see if one program is getting much less money than the others

24. If a manager were trying to explain the fundamental difference between traditional accounting theory and practice and the newer practice of managerial accounting, he would be MOST accurate if he said that

    24._

    A. traditional accounting practice focused on providing information for persons outside organizations, while managerial accounting focuses on providing information for people inside organizations

    B. traditional accounting practice focused on providing information for persons inside organizations while managerial accounting focuses on providing information for persons outside organizations

    C. managerial accounting is exclusively concerned with historical facts while traditional accounting stresses future projections exclusively

    D. traditional accounting practice is more budget-focused than managerial accounting

25. Which of the following formulas is used to determine the number of days required to process work?

    25._

    A. $\dfrac{\text{Employees x Daily Output}}{\text{Volume}}$ = Days to Process Work

    B. $\dfrac{\text{Volume x Daily Output}}{\text{Employees}}$ = Days to Process Work

    C. $\dfrac{\text{Volume}}{\text{Employees x Daily Output}}$ = Days to Process Work

    D. $\dfrac{\text{Employees x Volume}}{\text{Daily Output}}$ = Days to Process Work

KEY (CORRECT ANSWERS)

1.	C	11.	C
2.	C	12.	D
3.	D	13.	A
4.	B	14.	C
5.	D	15.	D
6.	D	16.	C
7.	D	17.	A
8.	A	18.	A
9.	B	19.	B
10.	C	20.	B

21.	D
22.	A
23.	B
24.	A
25.	C

TEST 3

DIRECTIONS: Each question or incomplete statement is followed by several suggested answers or completions. Select the one that BEST answers the question or completes the statement. *PRINT THE LETTER OF THE CORRECT ANSWER IN THE SPACE AT THE RIGHT.*

1. Electronic data processing equipment can produce more information faster than can be generated by any other means.
In view of this, the MOST important problem faced by management at present is to

    A. keep computers fully occupied
    B. find enough computer personnel
    C. assimilate and properly evaluate the information
    D. obtain funds to establish appropriate information systems

1.___

2. A well-designed management information system ESSENTIALLY provides each executive and manager the information he needs for

    A. determining computer time requirements
    B. planning and measuring results
    C. drawing a new organization chart
    D. developing a new office layout

2.___

3. It is generally agreed that management policies should be periodically reappraised and restated in accordance with current conditions.
Of the following, the approach which would be MOST effective in determining whether a policy should be revised is to

    A. conduct interviews with staff members at all levels in order to ascertain the relationship between the policy and actual practice
    B. make proposed revisions in the policy and apply it to current problems
    C. make up hypothetical situations using both the old policy and a revised version in order to make comparisons
    D. call a meeting of top level staff in order to discuss ways of revising the policy

3.___

4. Every manager has many occasions to lead a conference or participate in a conference of some sort.
Of the following statements that pertain to conferences and conference leadership, which is generally considered to be MOST valid?

    A. Since World War II, the trend has been toward fewer shared decisions and more conferences.
    B. The most important part of a conference leader's job is to direct discussion.
    C. In providing opportunities for group interaction, management should avoid consideration of its past management philosophy.
    D. A good administrator cannot lead a good conference if he is a poor public speaker.

4.___

5. Of the following, it is usually LEAST desirable for a conference leader to

    A. turn the question to the person who asked it
    B. summarize proceedings periodically
    C. make a practice of not repeating questions
    D. ask a question without indicating who is to reply

5.___

6. The behavioral school of management thought bases its beliefs on certain assumptions.   6.____
Which of the following is NOT a belief of this school of thought?

    A. People tend to seek and accept responsibility.
    B. Most people can be creative in solving problems.
    C. People prefer security above all else.
    D. Commitment is the most important factor in motivating people.

7. The one of the following objectives which would be LEAST appropriate as a major goal of   7.____
research in the field of human resources management is to

    A. predict future conditions, events, and manpower needs
    B. evaluate established policies, programs, and practices
    C. evaluate proposed policies, programs, and practices
    D. identify deficient organizational units and apply suitable penalties

8. Of the following general interviewing methods or techniques, the one that is USUALLY   8.____
considered to be effective in counseling, grievances, and appraisal interviews is the
_____ interview.

    A. directed   B. non-directed
    C. panel   D. patterned

9. The ESSENTIAL first phase of decision-making is   9.____

    A. finding alternative solutions
    B. making a diagnosis of the problem
    C. selecting the plan to follow
    D. analyzing and comparing alternative solutions

10. Assume that, in a certain organization, a situation has developed in which there is little   10.____
difference in status or authority between individuals.
Which of the following would be the MOST likely result with regard to communication in
this organization?

    A. Both the accuracy and flow of communication will be improved.
    B. Both the accuracy and flow of communication will substantially decrease.
    C. Employees will seek more formal lines of communication.
    D. Neither the flow nor the accuracy of communication will be improved over the
        former hierarchical structure.

11. The main function of many agency administrative offices is *information management*.   11.____
Information that is received by an administrative officer may be classified as active or
passive, depending upon whether or not it requires the recipient to take some action.
Of the following, the item received which is clearly the MOST active information is

    A. an appointment of a new staff member
    B. a payment voucher for a new desk
    C. a press release concerning a past city event
    D. the minutes of a staff meeting

12. Which one of the following sets BEST describes the general order in which to teach an operation to a new employee?

    A. Prepare, present, tryout, follow-up
    B. Prepare, test, tryout, re-test
    C. Present, test, tryout, follow-up
    D. Test, present, follow-up, re-test

12.__

13. Of the following, public employees may be separated from public service

    A. for the same reasons which are generally acceptable for discharging employees in private industry
    B. only under the most trying circumstances
    C. under procedures that are neither formalized nor subject to review
    D. solely in extreme cases involving offenses of gravest character

13.__

14. Of the following, the one LEAST considered to be a communication barrier is

    A. group feedback
    B. charged words
    C. selective perception
    D. symbolic meanings

14.__

15. Of the following ways for a manager to handle his appointments, the BEST way, according to experts in administration, generally is to

    A. schedule his own appointments and inform his secretary not to reserve his time without his approval
    B. encourage everyone to make appointments through his secretary and tell her when he makes his own appointments
    C. see no one who has not made a previous appointment
    D. permit anyone to see him without an appointment

15.__

16. Assume that a manager decides to examine closely one of five units under his supervision to uncover problems common to all five.
His research technique is MOST closely related to the method called

    A. experimentation
    B. simulation
    C. linear analysis
    D. sampling

16.__

17. If one views the process of management as a dynamic process, which one of the following functions is NOT a legitimate part of that process?

    A. Communication
    B. Decision-making
    C. Organizational slack
    D. Motivation

17.__

18. Which of the following would be the BEST statement of a budget-oriented purpose for a government administrator? To

    A. provide 200 hours of instruction in basic reading for 3500 adult illiterates at a cost of $1 million in the next fiscal year
    B. inform the public of adult educational programs
    C. facilitate the transfer to a city agency of certain functions of a federally-funded program which is being phased out
    D. improve the reading skills of the adult citizens in the city

18.__

19. Modern management philosophy and practices are changing to accommodate the   19._____
    expectations and motivations of organization personnel.
    Which of the following terms INCORRECTLY describes these newer managerial
    approaches?

    A. Rational management   B. Participative management
    C. Decentralization   D. Democratic supervision

20. Management studies support the hypothesis that, in spite of the tendency of employees   20._____
    to censor the information communicated to their supervisor, subordinates are MORE
    likely to communicate problem-oriented information upward when they have

    A. a long period of service in the organization
    B. a high degree of trust in the supervisor
    C. a high educational level
    D. low status on the organizational ladder

KEY (CORRECT ANSWERS)

1.	C		11.	A
2.	B		12.	A
3.	A		13.	A
4.	B		14.	A
5.	A		15.	B
6.	C		16.	D
7.	D		17.	C
8.	B		18.	A
9.	B		19.	A
10.	D		20.	B

INTERPRETING STATISTICAL DATA
GRAPHS, CHARTS AND TABLES
TEST 1

DIRECTIONS: Each question or incomplete statement is followed by several suggested answers or completions. Select the one that BEST answers the question or completes the statement. *PRINT THE LETTER OF THE CORRECT ANSWER IN THE SPACE AT THE RIGHT.*

Questions 1-8.

DIRECTIONS: Questions 1 through 8 are to be answered SOLELY on the basis of the information and chart given below.

The following chart shows expenses in five selected categories for a one-year period expressed as percentages of these same expenses during the previous year. The chart compares two different offices. In Office T(represented by ☐) a cost reduction program has oeen tested for the past year. The other office, Office Q(represented by ▨) served as a control, in that no special effort was made to reduce costs during the past year.

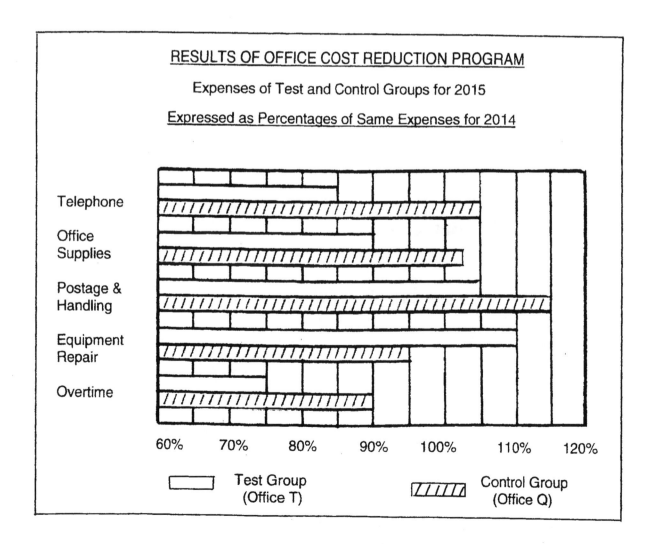

1. In Office T, which category of expense showed the GREATEST percentage reduction   1.____
    from 2014 to 2015?

    A. Telephone   B. Office supplies
    C. Postage and mailing   D. Overtime

2. In which expense category did Office T show the BEST results in percentage terms   2.____
    when compared to Office Q?

    A. Telephone   B. Office supplies
    C. Postage and mailing   D. Overtime

3. According to the above chart, the cost reduction program was LEAST effective for the   3.____
    expense category of

    A. Office supplies   B. Postage and mailing
    C. Equipment repair   D. Overtime

4. Office T's telephone costs went down during 2015 by APPROXIMATELY how many per-   4.____
    centage points?

    A. 15   B. 20   C. 85   D. 105

5. Which of the following changes occurred in expenses for Office Supplies in Office Q in   5.____
    the year 2015 as compared with the year 2014?
    They

    A. *increased* by more than 100%
    B. *remained* the same
    C. *decreased* by a few percentage points
    D. *increased* by a few percentage points

6. For which of the following expense categories do the results in Office T and the results in   6.____
    Office Q differ MOST NEARLY by 10 percentage points?

    A. Telephone   B. Postage and mailing
    C. Equipment repair   D. Overtime

7. In which expense category did Office Q's costs show the GREATEST percentage   7.____
    increase in 2015?

    A. Telephone   B. Office supplies
    C. Postage and mailing   D. Equipment repair

8. In Office T, by APPROXIMATELY what percentage did overtime expense change during   8.____
    the past year?
    It

    A. *increased* by 15%   B. *increased* by 75%
    C. *decreased* by 10%   D. *decreased* by 25%

KEY (CORRECT ANSWERS)

1. D
2. A
3. C
4. A

5. D
6. B
7. C
8. D

———

TEST 2

Questions 1-7.

DIRECTIONS: Questions 1 through 7 are to be answered SOLELY on the basis of the information contained in the graph below which relates to the work of a public agency.

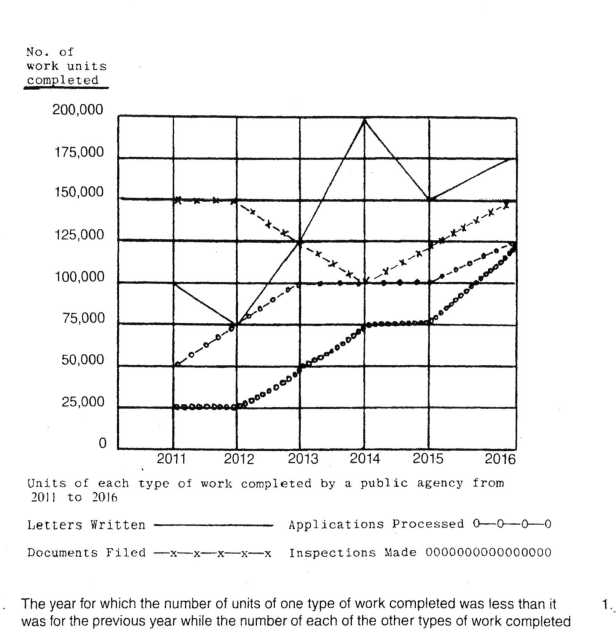

Units of each type of work completed by a public agency from 2011 to 2016

Letters Written —————————— Applications Processed O—O—O—O

Documents Filed —x—x—x—x—x Inspections Made OOOOOOOOOOOOOOO

1. The year for which the number of units of one type of work completed was less than it was for the previous year while the number of each of the other types of work completed was more than it was for the previous year was

1.____

   A. 2012   B. 2013   C. 2014   D. 2015

2. The number of letters written exceeded the number of applications processed by the same amount in _____ of the years.

2.____

   A. two   B. three   C. four   D. five

3. The year in which the number of each type of work completed was GREATER than in the preceding year was   3.____

    A. 2013   B. 2014   C. 2015   D. 2016

4. The number of applications processed and the number of documents filed were the SAME in   4.____

    A. 2012   B. 2013   C. 2014   D. 2015

5. The TOTAL number of units of work completed by the agency   5.____

    A. increased in each year after 2011
    B. decreased from the prior year in two of the years after 2011
    C. was the same in two successive years from 2011 to 2016
    D. was less in 2011 than in any of the following years

6. For the year in which the number of letters written was twice as high as it was in 2011, the number of documents filed was _____ it was in 2011.   6.____

    A. the same as
    B. two-thirds of what
    C. five-sixths of what
    D. one and one-half times what

7. The variable which was the MOST stable during the period 2011 through 2016 was   7.____

    A. Inspections Made   B. Letters Written
    C. Documents Filed   D. Applications Processed

KEY (CORRECT ANSWERS)

1.	B	5.	C
2.	B	6.	B
3.	D	7.	D
4.	C		

TEST 3

Questions 1-10.

DIRECTIONS: Questions 1 through 10 are to be answered SOLELY on the basis of the REPORT OF TELEPHONE CALLS table given below.

TABLE – REPORT OF TELEPHONE CALLS

Dept.	No. of Stations	No. of Employees	No. of Incoming Calls In 2014	2015	No. of Long Distance Calls In 2014	2015	No. of Divisions
I	11	40	3421	4292	72	54	5
II	36	330	10392	10191	75	78	18
III	53	250	85243	85084	103	98	8
IV	24	60	9675	10123	82	85	6
V	13	30	5208	5492	54	48	6
VI	25	35	7472	8109	86	90	5
VII	37	195	11412	11299	68	72	11
VIII	36	54	8467	8674	59	68	4
IX	163	306	294321	289968	289	321	13
X	40	83	9588	8266	93	89	5
XI	24	68	7867	7433	86	87	13
XII	50	248	10039	10208	101	95	30
XIII	10	230	7550	6941	28	21	10
XIV	25	103	14281	14392	48	40	5
XV	19	230	8475	9206	38	43	8
XVI	22	45	4684	5584	39	48	10
XVII	41	58	10102	9677	49	52	6
XVIII	82	106	106242	105899	128	132	10
XIX	6	13	2649	2498	35	29	2
XX	16	30	1395	1468	78	90	2

1. The department which had more than 106,000 incoming calls in 2014 but fewer than 250,000 is

   A. II   B. IX   C. XVIII   D. III

   1._____

2. The department which has fewer than 8 divisions and more than 100 but fewer than 300 employees is

   A. VII   B. XIV   C. XV   D. XVIII

   2._____

3. The department which had an increase in 2015 over 2014 in the number of both incoming and long distance calls but had an increase in long distance calls of not more than 3

   A. IV   B. VI   C. XVII   D. XVIII

   3._____

4. The department which had a decrease in the number of incoming calls in 2015 as compared to 2014 and has not less than 6 nor more than 7 divisions is

   A. IV   B. V   C. XVII   D. III

   4._____

5. The department which has more than 7 divisions and more than 200 employees but fewer than 19 stations is

   A. XV   B. III   C. XX   D. XIII

   5._____

6. The department having more than 10 divisions and fewer than 36 stations, which had an increase in long distance calls in 2015 over 2014, is

   A. XI   B. VII   C. XVI   D. XVIII

   6._____

7. The department which in 2015 had at least 7,250 incoming calls and a decrease in long distance calls from 2014 and has more than 50 stations is 　　7.____

    A. IX　　　　　B. XII　　　　　C. XVIII　　　　　D. III

8. The department which has fewer than 25 stations, fewer than 100 employees, 10 or more divisions, and showed an increase of at least 9 long distance calls in 2015 over 2014 is 　　8.____

    A. IX　　　　　B. XVI　　　　　C. XX　　　　　D. XIII

9. The department which has more than 50 but fewer than 125 employees and had more than 5,000 incoming calls in 2014 but not more than 10,000, and more than 60 long distance calls in 2015 but not more than 85, and has more than 24 stations is 　　9.____

    A. VIII　　　　　B. XIV　　　　　C. IV　　　　　D. XI

10. If the number of departments showing an increase in long distance calls in 2015 over 1999 exceeds the number showing a decrease in long distance calls in the same period, select the Roman numeral indicating the department having less than one station for each 10 employees, provided not more than 8 divisions are served by that department. If the number of departments showing an increase in long distance calls in 2015 over 2014 does not exceed the number showing a decrease in long distance calls in the same period, select the Roman numeral indicating the department having the SMALLEST number of incoming calls in 2015. 　　10.____

    A. III　　　　　B. XIII　　　　　C. XV　　　　　D. XX

KEY (CORRECT ANSWERS)

1.	C	6.	A
2.	B	7.	D
3.	A	8.	B
4.	C	9.	A
5.	D	10.	C

TEST 4

Questions 1-6.

DIRECTIONS: Questions 1 through 6 are to be answered SOLELY on the basis of the information given in the chart below. This chart shows the results of a study made of the tasks performed by a stenographer during one day. Included in the chart are the time at which she started a certain task and, under the particular heading, the amount of time, in minutes, she took to complete the task, and explanations of telephone calls and miscellaneous activities. NOTE: The time spent at lunch should not be included in any of your calculations.

PAMELA JOB STUDY

NAME: Pamela Donald DATE: 9/26
JOB TITLE: Stenographer
DIVISION: Stenographic Pool

Time of Start of Task	TASKS PERFORMED						Explanations of Telephone Calls and Miscellaneous Activities
	Taking Dicta-tion	Typ-ing	Fil-ing	Tele-phone Work	Hand-ling Mail	Misc. Acti-vities	
9:00					22		
9:22						13	Picking up supplies
9:35						15	Cleaning typewriter
9:50	11						
10:01		30					
10:31				8			Call to Agency A
10:39	12						
10:51			10				
11:01				7			Call from Agency B
11:08		30					
11:38	10						
11:48				12			Call from Agency C
12:00	L U N C H						
1:00					28		
1:28	13						
1:41 2:13		32		12			Call to Agency B
X			15				
Y		50					
3:30	10						
3:40		21					
4:01				9			Call from Agency A
4:10	35						
4:45		9					
4:54						6	Cleaning up desk

SAMPLE QUESTION:

The total amount of time spent on miscellaneous activities in the morning is exactly equal to the total amount of time spent

    A. filing in the morning
    B. handling mail in the afternoon
    C. miscellaneous activities in the afternoon
    D. handling mail in the morning

Explanation of answer to sample question:

The total amount of time spent on miscellaneous activities in the morning equals 28 minutes (13 minutes for picking up supplies plus 15 minutes for cleaning the typewriter); and since it takes 28 minutes to handle mail in the afternoon, the answer is B.

1. The time labeled Y at which the stenographer started a typing assignment was   1._____

    A. 2:15   B. 2:25   C. 2:40   D. 2:50

2. The ratio of time spent on all incoming calls to time spent on all outgoing calls for the day   2._____
was

    A. 5:7   B. 5:12   C. 7:5   D. 7:12

3. Of the following combinations of tasks, which ones take up exactly 80% of the total time   3._____
spent on Tasks Performed during the day?

    A. Typing, filing, telephone work, and handling mail
    B. Taking dictation, filing, and miscellaneous activities
    C. Taking dictation, typing, handling mail, and miscellaneous activities
    D. Taking dictation, typing, filing, and telephone work

4. The total amount of time spent transcribing or typing work is how much MORE than the   4._____
total amount of time spent in taking dictation?

    A. 55 minutes   B. 1 hour
    C. 1 hour 10 minutes   D. 1 hour 25 minutes

5. The GREATEST number of shifts in activities occurred between the times of   5._____

    A. 9:00 A.M. and 10:31 A.M.
    B. 9:35 A.M. and 11:01 A.M.
    C. 10:31 A.M. and 12:00 Noon
    D. 3:30 P.M. and 5:00 P.M.

6. The total amount of time spent on taking dictation in the morning plus the total amount of   6._____
time spent on filing in the afternoon is exactly EQUAL to the total amount of time spent
on

    A. typing in the afternoon minus the total amount of time spent on telephone work in
the afternoon
    B. typing in the morning plus the total amount of time spent on miscellaneous activities in the afternoon
    C. dictation in the afternoon plus the total amount of time spent on filing in the morning
    D. typing in the afternoon minus the total amount of time spent on handling mail in the morning

KEY (CORRECT ANSWERS)

    1. C   4. B
    2. C   5. C
    3. D   6. D

TEST 5

Questions 1-8.

DIRECTIONS: Questions 1 through 8 are to be answered SOLELY on the basis of the information given in the table below.

	Bronx		Brooklyn		Manhattan		Queens		Richmond	
	May	June	May	June	May	June	May	June	May	June
Number of Clerks in Office Assigned To Issue Applications for Licenses	3	4	6	8	6	8	3	5	3	4
Number of Licenses Issued	950	1010	1620	1940	1705	2025	895	1250	685	975
Amount Collected in License Fees	$42,400	$52,100	$77,600	$94,500	583,700	$98,800	$39,300	$65,500	$30,600	$48,200
Number of Inspectors	4	5	6	7	7	8	4	5	2	4
Number of Inspections Made	420	450	630	710	690	740	400	580	320	440
Number of Violations Found as a Result of Inspections	211	153	352	378	320	385	256	304	105	247

1. Of the following statements, the one which is NOT accurate on the basis of an inspection of the information contained in the table is that, for each office, the increase from May to June in the number of

    A. inspectors was accompanied by an increase in the number of inspections made
    B. licenses issued was accompanied by an increase in the amount collected in license fees
    C. inspections made was accompanied by an increase in the number of violations found
    D. licenses issued was accompanied by an increase in the number of clerks assigned to issue applications for licenses

2. The TOTAL number of licenses issued by all five offices in the Division in May was

    A. 4800   B. 5855   C. 6865   D. 7200

1. ___

2. ___

3. The total number of inspectors in all five borough offices in June exceeded the number in   3.____
   May by MOST NEARLY

   A. 21%   B. 26%   C. 55%   D. 70%

4. In the month of June, the number of violations found per inspection made was the HIGH-   4.____
   EST in

   A. Brooklyn   B. Manhattan   C. Queens   D. Richmond

5. In the month of May, the average number of inspections made by an inspector in the   5.____
   Bronx was the same as the average number of inspections made by an inspector in

   A. Brooklyn   B. Manhattan   C. Queens   D. Richmond

6. Assume that in June all of the inspectors in the Division spent 7 hours a day making   6.____
   inspections on each of the 21 working days in the month.
   Then the average amount of time that an inspector in the Manhattan office spent on an
   inspection that month was MOST NEARLY

   A. 2 hours   B. 1 hour and 35 minutes
   C. 1 hour and 3 minutes   D. 38 minutes

7. If an average fine of $100 was imposed for a violation found by the Division, what was the   7.____
   TOTAL amount in fines imposed for all the violations found by the Division in May?

   A. $124,400   B. $133,500   C. $146,700   D. $267,000

8. Assume that the amount collected in license fees by the entire Division in May was 80   8.____
   percent of the amount collected by the entire Division in April.
   How much was collected by the entire Division in April?

   A. $218,880   B. $328,320   C. $342,000   D. $410,400

KEY (CORRECT ANSWERS)

1.	C	5.	A
2.	B	6.	B
3.	B	7.	A
4.	D	8.	C

TEST 6

Questions 1-8.

DIRECTIONS: Questions 1 through 8 are to be answered SOLELY on the basis of the information contained in the chart and table shown below, which relate to Bureau X in a certain public agency. The chart shows the percentage of the bureau's annual expenditures spent on equipment, supplies, and salaries for each of the years 2012-2016. The table shows the bureau's annual expenditures for each of the years 2012-2016.

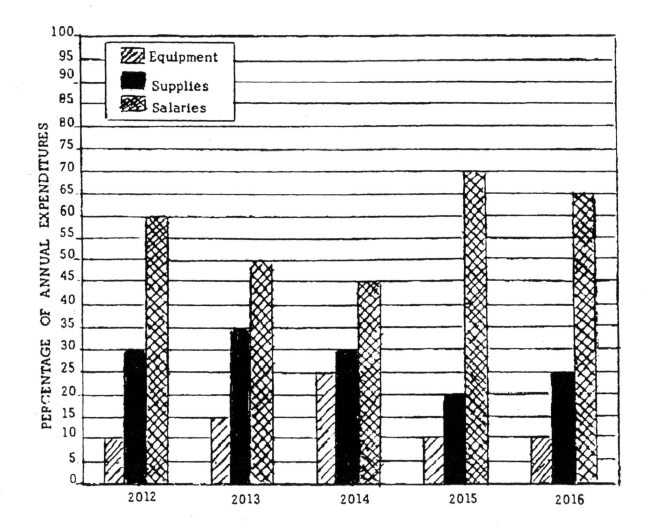

The bureau's annual expenditures for the years 2012-2016 are shown in the following table:

YEAR	EXPENDITURES
2012	$ 8,000,000
2013	$12,000,000
2014	$15,000,000
2015	$10,000,000
2016	$12,000,000

Equipment, supplies, and salaries were the only three categories for which the bureau spent money.

Candidates may find it useful to arrange their computations on their scratch paper in an orderly manner since the correct computations for one question may also be helpful in answering another question.

1. The information contained in the chart and table is sufficient to determine the   1.____

    A. average annual salary of an employee in the bureau in 2013
    B. decrease in the amount of money spent on supplies in the bureau in 2012 from the amount spent in the preceding year
    C. changes between 2014 and 2015 in the prices of supplies bought by the bureau
    D. increase in the amount of money spent on salaries in the bureau in 2016 over the amount spent in the preceding year

2. If the percentage of expenditures for salaries in one year is added to the percentage of expenditures for equipment in that year, a total of two percentages for that year is obtained.   2.____
The two years for which this total is the SAME are

    A. 2012 and 2014   B. 2013 and 2015
    C. 2012 and 2015   D. 2013 and 2016

3. Of the following, the year in which the bureau spent the GREATEST amount of money on supplies was   3.____

    A. 2016   B. 2014   C. 2008   D. 2012

4. Of the following years, the one in which there was the GREATEST increase over the preceding year in the amount of money spent on salaries is   4.____

    A. 2015   B. 2016   C. 2013   D. 2014

5. Of the bureau's expenditures for equipment in 2016, one-third was used for the purchase of mailroom equipment and the remainder was spent on miscellaneous office equipment. How much did the bureau spend on miscellaneous office equipment in 2016?   5.____

    A. $4,000,000   B. $400,000
    C. $8,000,000   D. $800,000

6. If there were 120 employees in the bureau in 2015, then the average annual salary paid to the employees in that year was MOST NEARLY   6.____

    A. $43,450   B. $49,600   C. $58,350   D. $80,800

7. In 2014, the bureau had 125 employees.   7.____
If 20 of the employees earned an average annual salary of $80,000, then the average salary of the other 105 employees was MOST NEARLY

    A. $49,000   B. $64,000   C. $41,000   D. $54,000

8. Assume that the bureau estimated that the amount of money it would spend on supplies   8._____
in 2017 would be the same as the amount it spent on that category in 2016. Similarly, the
bureau estimated that the amount of money it would spend on equipment in 2017 would
be the same as the amount it spent on that category in 2016. However, the bureau estimated that in 2017 the amount it would spend on salaries would be 10 percent higher
than the amount it spent on that category in 2016.
The percentage of its annual expenditures that the bureau estimated it would spend on
supplies in 2017 is MOST NEARLY

    A. 27.5%   B. 23.5%   C. 22.5%   D. 25%

KEY (CORRECT ANSWERS)

1.	D		5.	D
2.	A		6.	C
3.	B		7.	A
4.	C		8.	B

PREPARING WRITTEN MATERIAL

EXAMINATION SECTION
TEST 1

DIRECTIONS: Each of the sentences in the Tests that follow may be classified under one of the following four categories:

      A. *Faulty* because of incorrect grammar or word usage
      B. *Faulty* because of incorrect punctuation
      C. *Faulty* because of incorrect capitalization or incorrect spelling
      D. *Correct*

Examine each sentence carefully to determine under which of the above four options it is best classified. Then, in the space to the right, print the capital letter preceding the option which is the best of the four suggested above.

(Note that each faulty sentence contains but one type of error. Consider a sentence to be correct if it contains none of the types of errors mentioned, even though there may be other correct ways of expressing the same thought.)

1.   He sent the notice to the clerk who you hired yesterday.   1._____

2.   It must be admitted, however that you were not informed of this change.   2._____

3.   Only the employees who have served in this grade for at least two years are eligible for promotion.   3._____

4.   The work was divided equally between she and Mary.   4._____

5.   He thought that you were not available at that time.   5._____

6.   When the messenger returns; please give him this package.   6._____

7.   The new secretary prepared, typed, addressed, and delivered, the notices.   7._____

8.   Walking into the room, his desk can be seen at the rear.   8._____

9.   Although John has worked here longer than She, he produces a smaller amount of work.   9._____

10.   She said she could of typed this report yesterday.   10._____

11.   Neither one of these procedures are adequate for the efficient performance of this task.   11._____

12.   The typewriter is the tool of the typist; the cash register, the tool of the cashier.   12._____

13.   "The assignment must be completed as soon as possible" said the supervisor.   13._____

14.   As you know, office handbooks are issued to all new Employees.   14._____

15.   Writing a speech is sometimes easier than to deliver it before an audience.   15._____

16.   Mr. Brown our accountant, will audit the accounts next week.   16._____

17. Give the assignment to whomever is able to do it most efficiently.   17.__

18. The supervisor expected either your or I to file these reports.   18.__

KEY (CORRECT ANSWERS)

1.	A		10.	A
2.	B		11.	A
3.	D		12.	C
4.	A		13.	B
5.	D		14.	C
6.	B		15.	A
7.	B		16.	B
8.	A		17.	A
9.	C		18.	A

TEST 2

DIRECTIONS: Each of the sentences in the Tests that follow may be classified under one of the following four categories:
- A. *Faulty* because of incorrect grammar or word usage
- B. *Faulty* because of incorrect punctuation
- C. *Faulty* because of incorrect capitalization or incorrect spelling
- D. *Correct*

Examine each sentence carefully to determine under which of the above four options it is best classified. Then, in the space to the right, print the capital letter preceding the option which is the best of the four suggested above.

(Note that each faulty sentence contains but one type of error. Consider a sentence to be correct if it contains none of the types of errors mentioned, even though there may be other correct ways of expressing the same thought.)

1. The fire apparently started in the storeroom, which is usually locked.   1._____

2. On approaching the victim, two bruises were noticed by this officer.   2._____

3. The officer, who was there examined the report with great care.   3._____

4. Each employee in the office had a seperate desk.   4._____

5. All employees including members of the clerical staff, were invited to the lecture.   5._____

6. The suggested Procedure is similar to the one now in use.   6._____

7. No one was more pleased with the new procedure than the chauffeur.   7._____

8. He tried to persaude her to change the procedure.   8._____

9. The total of the expenses charged to petty cash were high.   9._____

10. An understanding between him and I was finally reached.   10._____

KEY (CORRECT ANSWERS)

1.	D		6.	C
2.	A		7.	D
3.	B		8.	C
4.	C		9.	A
5.	B		10.	A

———

TEST 3

DIRECTIONS: Each of the sentences in the Tests that follow may be classified under one of the following four categories:
A. *Faulty* because of incorrect grammar or word usage
B. *Faulty* because of incorrect punctuation
C. *Faulty* because of incorrect capitalization or incorrect spelling
D. *Correct*

Examine each sentence carefully to determine under which of the above four options it is best classified. Then, in the space to the right, print the capital letter preceding the option which is the best of the four suggested above.

(Note that each faulty sentence contains but one type of error. Consider a sentence to be correct if it contains none of the types of errors mentioned, even though there may be other correct ways of expressing the same thought.)

1. They told both he and I that the prisoner had escaped.   1._____

2. Any superior officer, who, disregards the just complaints of his subordinates, is remiss in   2._____
   the performance of his duty.

3. Only those members of the national organization who resided in the Middle West   3._____
   attended the conference in Chicago.

4. We told him to give the investigation assignment to whoever was available.   4._____

5. Please do not disappoint and embarass us by not appearing in court.   5._____

6. Although the officer's speech proved to be entertaining, the topic was not relevent to the   6._____
   main theme of the conference.

7. In February all new officers attended a training course in which they were learned in their 7._____
   principal duties and the fundamental operating procedures of the department.

8. I personally seen inmate Jones threaten inmates Smith and Green with bodily harm if   8._____
   they refused to participate in the plot.

9. To the layman, who on a chance visit to the prison observes everything functioning   9._____
   smoothly, the maintenance of prison discipline may seem to be a relatively easily realiz-
   able objective.

10. The prisoners in cell block fourty were forbidden to sit on the cell cots during the recre- 10._____
    ation hour.

_____

KEY (CORRECT ANSWERS)

1. A
2. B
3. C
4. D
5. C

6. C
7. A
8. A
9. D
10. C

TEST 4

DIRECTIONS: Each of the sentences in the Tests that follow may be classified under one of the following four categories:
   A.   *Faulty* because of incorrect grammar or word usage
   B.   *Faulty* because of incorrect punctuation
   C.   *Faulty* because of incorrect capitalization or incorrect spelling
   D.   *Correct*

   Examine each sentence carefully to determine under which of the above four options it is best classified. Then, in the space to the right, print the capital letter preceding the option which is the best of the four suggested above.

   (Note that each faulty sentence contains but one type of error. Consider a sentence to be correct if it contains none of the types of errors mentioned, even though there may be other correct ways of expressing the same thought.)

1.   I cannot encourage you any.   1.____

2.   You always look well in those sort of clothes.   2.____

3.   Shall we go to the park?   3.____

4.   The man whome he introduced was Mr. Carey.   4.____

5.   She saw the letter laying here this morning.   5.____

6.   It should rain before the Afternoon is over.   6.____

7.   They have already went home.   7.____

8.   That Jackson will be elected is evident.   8.____

9.   He does not hardly approve of us.   9.____

10.   It was he, who won the prize.   10.____

KEY (CORRECT ANSWERS)

1.	A	6.	C
2.	A	7.	A
3.	D	8.	D
4.	C	9.	A
5.	A	10.	B

———

TEST 5

DIRECTIONS: Each of the sentences in the Tests that follow may be classified under one of the following four categories:
   A.   *Faulty* because of incorrect grammar or word usage
   B.   *Faulty* because of incorrect punctuation
   C.   *Faulty* because of incorrect capitalization or incorrect spelling
   D.   *Correct*

   Examine each sentence carefully to determine under which of the above four options it is best classified. Then, in the space to the right, print the capital letter preceding the option which is the best of the four suggested above.

   (Note that each faulty sentence contains but one type of error. Consider a sentence to be correct if it contains none of the types of errors mentioned, even though there may be other correct ways of expressing the same thought.)

1.   Shall we go to the park.   1._____

2.   They are, alike, in this particular way.   2._____

3.   They gave the poor man sume food when he knocked on the door.   3._____

4.   I regret the loss caused by the error.   4._____

5.   The students' will have a new teacher.   5._____

6.   They sweared to bring out all the facts.   6._____

7.   He decided to open a branch store on 33rd street.   7._____

8.   His speed is equal and more than that of a racehorse.   8._____

9.   He felt very warm on that Summer day.   9._____

10.   He was assisted by his friend, who lives in the next house.   10._____

———

KEY (CORRECT ANSWERS)

1.	B	6.	A
2.	B	7.	C
3.	C	8.	A
4.	D	9.	C
5.	B	10.	D

———

TEST 6

DIRECTIONS: Each of the sentences in the Tests that follow may be classified under one of the following four categories:
- A. *Faulty* because of incorrect grammar or word usage
- B. *Faulty* because of incorrect punctuation
- C. *Faulty* because of incorrect capitalization or incorrect spelling
- D. *Correct*

Examine each sentence carefully to determine under which of the above four options it is best classified. Then, in the space to the right, print the capital letter preceding the option which is the best of the four suggested above.

(Note that each faulty sentence contains but one type of error. Consider a sentence to be correct if it contains none of the types of errors mentioned, even though there may be other correct ways of expressing the same thought.)

1. The climate of New York is colder than California.   1._____

2. I shall wait for you on the corner.   2._____

3. Did we see the boy who, we think, is the leader.   3._____

4. Being a modest person, John seldom talks about his invention.   4._____

5. The gang is called the smith street boys.   5._____

6. He seen the man break into the store.   6._____

7. We expected to lay still there for quite a while.   7._____

8. He is considered to be the Leader of his organization.   8._____

9. Although I recieved an invitation, I won't go.   9._____

10. The letter must be here some place.   10._____

KEY (CORRECT ANSWERS)

1.	A	6.	A
2.	D	7.	A
3.	B	8.	C
4.	D	9.	C
5.	C	10.	A

———

TEST 7

DIRECTIONS: Each of the sentences in the Tests that follow may be classified under one of the following four categories:
- A. *Faulty* because of incorrect grammar or word usage
- B. *Faulty* because of incorrect punctuation
- C. *Faulty* because of incorrect capitalization or incorrect spelling
- D. *Correct*

    Examine each sentence carefully to determine under which of the above four options it is best classified. Then, in the space to the right, print the capital letter preceding the option which is the best of the four suggested above.

    (Note that each faulty sentence contains but one type of error. Consider a sentence to be correct if it contains none of the types of errors mentioned, even though there may be other correct ways of expressing the same thought.)

1. I though it to be he.   1.____

2. We expect to remain here for a long time.   2.____

3. The committee was agreed.   3.____

4. Two-thirds of the building are finished.   4.____

5. The water was froze.   5.____

6. Everyone of the salesmen must supply their own car.   6.____

7. Who is the author of Gone With the Wind?   7.____

8. He marched on and declaring that he would never surrender.   8.____

9. Who shall I say called?   9.____

10. Everyone has left but they.   10.____

———

KEY (CORRECT ANSWERS)

1.	A		6.	A
2.	D		7.	B
3.	D		8.	A
4.	A		9.	D
5.	A		10.	D

———

TEST 8

DIRECTIONS: Each of the sentences in the Tests that follow may be classified under one of the following four categories:
  - A. *Faulty* because of incorrect grammar or word usage
  - B. *Faulty* because of incorrect punctuation
  - C. *Faulty* because of incorrect capitalization or incorrect spelling
  - D. *Correct*

Examine each sentence carefully to determine under which of the above four options it is best classified. Then, in the space to the right, print the capital letter preceding the option which is the best of the four suggested above.

(Note that each faulty sentence contains but one type of error. Consider a sentence to be correct if it contains none of the types of errors mentioned, even though there may be other correct ways of expressing the same thought.)

1. Who did we give the order to?   1.____

2. Send your order in immediately.   2.____

3. I believe I paid the Bill.   3.____

4. I have not met but one person.   4.____

5. Why aren't Tom, and Fred, going to the dance?   5.____

6. What reason is there for him not going?   6.____

7. The seige of Malta was a tremendous event.   7.____

8. I was there yesterday I assure you.   8.____

9. Your ukelele is better than mine.   9.____

10. No one was there only Mary.   10.____

———

KEY (CORRECT ANSWERS)

1.	A		6.	A
2.	D		7.	C
3.	C		8.	B
4.	A		9.	C
5.	B		10.	A

———

TEST 9

DIRECTIONS: In each of the following groups of sentences, one of the four sentences is faulty in grammar, punctuation, or capitalization. Select the incorrect sentence in each case.

1.
   A. If you had stood at home and done your homework, you would not have failed in arithmetic.
   B. Her affected manner annoyed every member of the audience.
   C. How will the new law affect our income taxes?
   D. The plants were not affected by the long, cold winter, but they succumbed to the drought of summer.

   1._____

2.
   A. He is one of the most able men who have been in the Senate.
   B. It is he who is to blame for the lamentable mistake.
   C. Haven't you a helpful suggestion to make at this time?
   D. The money was robbed from the blind man's cup.

   2._____

3.
   A. The amount of children in this school is steadily increasing.
   B. After taking an apple from the table, she went out to play.
   C. He borrowed a dollar from me.
   D. I had hoped my brother would arrive before me.

   3._____

4.
   A. Whom do you think I hear from every week?
   B. Who do you think is the right man for the job?
   C. Who do you think I found in the room?
   D. He is the man whom we considered a good candidate for the presidency.

   4._____

5.
   A. Quietly the puppy laid down before the fireplace.
   B. You have made your bed; now lie in it.
   C. I was badly sunburned because I had lain too long in the sun.
   D. I laid the doll on the bed and left the room.

   5._____

KEY (CORRECT ANSWERS)

1. A
2. D
3. A
4. C
5. A

———

PREPARING WRITTEN MATERIAL

PARAGRAPH REARRANGEMENT
COMMENTARY

The sentences which follow are in scrambled order. You are to rearrange them in proper order and indicate the letter choice containing the correct answer at the space at the right.

Each group of sentences in this section is actually a paragraph presented in scrambled order. Each sentence in the group has a place in that paragraph; no sentence is to be left out. You are to read each group of sentences and decide upon the best order in which to put the sentences so as to form as well-organized paragraph.

The questions in this section measure the ability to solve a problem when all the facts relevant to its solution are not given.

More specifically, certain positions of responsibility and authority require the employee to discover connections between events sometimes, apparently, unrelated. In order to do this, the employee will find it necessary to correctly infer that unspecified events have probably occurred or are likely to occur. This ability becomes especially important when action must be taken on incomplete information.

Accordingly, these questions require competitors to choose among several suggested alternatives, each of which presents a different sequential arrangement of the events. Competitors must choose the MOST logical of the suggested sequences.

In order to do so, they may be required to draw on general knowledge to infer missing concepts or events that are essential to sequencing the given events. Competitors should be careful to infer only what is essential to the sequence. The plausibility of the wrong alternatives will always require the inclusion of unlikely events or of additional chains of events which are NOT essential to sequencing the given events.

It's very important to remember that you are looking for the best of the four possible choices, and that the best choice of all may not even be one of the answers you're given to choose from.

There is no one right way to solve these problems. Many people have found it helpful to first write out the order of the sentences, as they would have arranged them, on their scrap paper before looking at the possible answers. If their optimum answer is there, this can save them some time. If it isn't, this method can still give insight into solving the problem. Others find it most helpful to just go through each of the possible choices, contrasting each as they go along. You should use whatever method feels comfortable, and works, for you.

While most of these types of questions are not that difficult, we've added a higher percentage of the difficult type, just to give you more practice. Usually there are only one or two questions on this section that contain such subtle distinctions that you're unable to answer confidently, and you then may find yourself stuck deciding between two possible choices, neither of which you're sure about.

———

Preparing Written Material

EXAMINATION SECTION
TEST 1

DIRECTIONS: The following groups of sentences need to be arranged in an order that makes sense. Select the letter preceding the sequence that represents the best sentence order. *PRINT THE LETTER OF THE CORRECT ANSWER IN THE SPACE AT THE RIGHT.*

Question 1   1.____

1. The ostrich egg shell's legendary toughness makes it an excellent substitute for certain types of dishes or dinnerware, and in parts of Africa ostrich shells are cut and decorated for use as containers for water.
2. Since prehistoric times, people have used the enormous egg of the ostrich as a part of their diet, a practice which has required much patience and hard work-to hard-boil an ostrich egg takes about four hours.
3. Opening the egg's shell, which is rock hard and nearly an inch thick, requires heavy tools, such as a saw or chisel; from inside, a baby ostrich must use a hornlike projection on its beak as a miniature pick-axe to escape from the egg.
4. The offspring of all higher-order animals originate from single egg cells that are carried by mothers, and most of these eggs are relatively small, often microscopic.
5. The egg of the African ostrich, however, weighs a massive thirty pounds, making it the largest single cell on earth, and a common object of human curiosity and wonder.

The best order is

A. 5 4 1 2 3
B. 1 4 5 3 2
C. 4 2 3 5 1
D. 4 5 2 3 1

Question 2   2.____

1. Typically only a few feet high on the open sea, individual tsunami have been known to circle the entire globe two or three times if their progress is not interrupted, but are not usually dangerous until they approach the shallow water that surrounds land masses.
2. Some of the most terrifying and damaging hazards caused by earthquakes are tsunami, which were once called "tidal waves"— a poorly chosen name, since these waves have nothing to do with tides.
3. Then a wave, slowed by the sudden drag on the lower part of its moving water column, will pile upon itself, sometimes reaching a height of over 100 feet.
4. Tsunami (Japanese for "great harbor wave") are seismic waves that are caused by earthquakes near oceanic trenches, and once triggered, can travel up to 600 miles an hour on the open ocean.
5. A land-shoaling tsunami is capable of extraordinary destruction; some tsunami have deposited large boats miles inland, washed out two-foot-thick seawalls, and scattered locomotive trains over long distances.

The best order is

A. 4 1 3 2 5
B. 1 3 4 2 5
C. 5 1 3 2 4
D. 2 4 1 3 5

Question 3

3._

1. Soon, by the 1940's, jazz was the most popular type of music among American intellectuals and college students.
2. In the early days of jazz, it was considered "lowdown" music, or music that was played only in rough, disreputable bars and taverns.
3. However, jazz didn't take long to develop from early ragtime melodies into more complex, sophisticated forms, such as Charlie Parker's "bebop" style of jazz.
4. After charismatic band leaders such as Duke Ellington and Count Basic brought jazz to a larger audience, and jazz continued to evolve into more complicated forms, white audiences began to accept and even to enjoy the new American art form.
5. Many white Americans, who then dictated the tastes of society, were wary of music that was played almost exclusively in black clubs in the poorer sections of cities and towns.

The best order is

A. 5 4 3 2 1
B. 2 5 3 4 1
C. 4 5 3 1 2
D. 1 2 4 3 5

Question 4

4._

1. Then, hanging in a windless place, the magnetized end of the needle would always point to the south.
2. The needle could then be balanced on the rim of a cup, or the edge of a fingernail, but this balancing act was hard to maintain, and the needle often fell off.
3. Other needles would point to the north, and it was important for any traveler finding his way with a compass to remember which kind of magnetized needle he was carrying.
4. To make some of the earliest compasses in recorded history, ancient Chinese "magicians" would rub a needle with a piece of magnetized iron called a lodestone.
5. A more effective method of keeping the needle free to swing with its magnetic pull was to attach a strand of silk to the center of the needle with a tiny piece of wax.

The best order is

A. 4 2 5 1 3
B. 4 3 5 2 1
C. 4 5 2 1 3
D. 4 1 3 5 2

Question 5

5.____

1. The now-famous first mate of the *HMS Bounty*, Fletcher Christian, founded one of the world's most peculiar civilizations in 1790.
2. The men knew they had just committed a crime for which they could be hanged, so they set sail for Pitcairn, a remote, abandoned island in the far eastern region of the Polynesian archipelago, accompanied by twelve Polynesian women and six men.
3. In a mutiny that has become legendary, Christian and the others forced Captain Bligh into a lifeboat and set him adrift off the coast of Tonga in April of 1789.
4. In early 1790, the *Bounty* landed at Pitcairn Island, where the men lived out the rest of their lives and founded an isolated community which to this day includes direct descendants of Christian and the other crewmen.
5. The *Bounty,* commanded by Captain William Bligh, was in the middle of a global voyage, and Christian and his shipmates had come to the conclusion that Bligh was a reckless madman who would lead them to their deaths unless they took the ship from him.

The best order is

A. 4 5 3 2 1
B. 1 3 5 2 4
C. 1 5 3 2 4
D. 3 1 5 4 2

Question 6

6.____

1. But once the vines had been led to make orchids, the flowers had to be carefully hand-pollinated, because unpollinated orchids usually lasted less than a day, wilting and dropping off the vine before it had even become dark.
2. The Totonac farmers discovered that looping a vine back around once it reached a five-foot height on its host tree would cause the vine to flower.
3. Though they knew how to process the fruit pods and extract vanilla's flavoring agent, the Totonacs also knew that a wild vanilla vine did not produce abundant flowers or fruit.
4. Wild vines climbed along the trunks and canopies of trees, and this constant upward growth diverted most of the vine's energy to making leaves instead of the orchid flowers that, once pollinated, would produce the flavorful pods.
5. Hundreds of years before vanilla became a prized food flavoring in Europe and the Western World, the Totonac Indians of the Mexican Gulf Coast were skilled cultivators of the vanilla vine, whose fruit they literally worshipped as a goddess.

The best order is

A. 2 3 4 1 5
B. 2 4 3 1 5
C. 5 3 4 2 1
D. 3 4 1 2 5

Question 7

7.___

1. Once airborne, the spider is at the mercy of the air currents—usually the spider takes a brief journey, traveling close to the ground, but some have been found in air samples collected as high as 10,000 feet, or been reported landing on ships far out at sea.
2. Once a young spider has hatched, it must leave the environment into which it was born as quickly as possible, in order to avoid competing with its hundreds of brothers and sisters for food.
3. The silk rises into warm air currents, and as soon as the pull feels adequate the spider lets go and drifts up into the air, suspended from the silk strand in the same way that a person might parasail.
4. To help young spiders do this, many species have adapted a practice known as "aerial dispersal," or, in common speech, "ballooning."
5. A spider that wants to leave its surroundings quickly will climb to the top of a grass stem or twig, face into the wind, and aim its back end into the air, releasing a long stream of silk from the glands near the tip of its abdomen.

The best order is

    A. 5 4 2 3 1
    B. 5 2 4 1 3
    C. 2 5 4 3 1
    D. 2 4 5 3 1

Question 8

8.___

1. For about a year, Tycho worked at a castle in Prague with a scientist named Johannes Kepler, but their association was cut short by another argument that drove Kepler out of the castle, to later develop, on his own, the theory of planetary orbits.
2. Tycho found life without a nose embarrassing, so he made a new nose for himself out of silver, which reportedly remained glued to his face for the rest of his life.
3. Tycho Brahe, the 17th-century Danish astronomer, is today more famous for his odd and arrogant personality than for any contribution he has made to our knowledge of the stars and planets.
4. Early in his career, as a student at Rostock University, Tycho got into an argument with the another student about who was the better mathematician, and the two became so angry that the argument turned into a sword fight, during which Tycho's nose was sliced off.
5. Later in his life, Tycho's arrogance may have kept him from playing a part in one of the greatest astronomical discoveries in history: the elliptical orbits of the solar system's planets.

The best order is

    A. 1 4 2 3 5
    B. 4 2 3 5 1
    C. 4 2 1 3 5
    D. 3 4 2 5 1

Question 9

9._____

1. The processionaries are so used to this routine that if a person picks up the end of a silk line and brings it back to the origin—creating a closed circle—the caterpillars may travel around and around for days, sometimes starving ar freezing, without changing course.

2. Rather than relying on sight or sound, the other caterpillars, who are lined up end-to-end behind the leader, travel to and from their nests by walking on this silk line, and each will reinforce it by laying down its own marking line as it passes over.

3. In order to insure the safety of individuals, the processionary caterpillar nests in a tree with dozens of other caterpillars, and at night, when it is safest, they all leave together in search of food.

4. The processionary caterpillar of the European continent is a perfect illustration of how much some insect species rely on instinct in their daily routines.

5. As they leave their nests, the processionaries form a single-file line behind a leader who spins and lays out a silk line to mark the chosen path.

The best order is

A. 4 3 5 2 1
B. 3 5 4 2 1
C. 3 5 2 1 4
D. 4 5 3 1 2

Question 10

10._____

1. Often, the child is also given a handcrafted walker or push cart, to provide support for its first upright explorations.

2. In traditional Indian families, a child's first steps are celebrated as a ceremonial event, rooted in ancient myth.

3. These carts are often intricately designed to resemble the chariot of Krishna, an important figure in Indian mythology.

4. The sound of these anklet bells is intended to mimic the footsteps of the legendary child Rama, who is celebrated in devotional songs throughout India.

5. When the child's parents see that the child is ready to begin walking, they will fit it with specially designed ankle bracelets, adorned with gently ringing bells.

The best order is

A. 2 3 4 1 5
B. 2 5 3 1 4
C. 5 4 1 3 2
D. 5 3 2 1 4

Question 11   11.

1. The settlers planted Osage orange all across Middle America, and today long lines and rectangles of Osage orange trees can still be seen on the prairies, running along the former boundaries of farms that no longer exist.
2. After trying sod walls and water-filled ditches with no success, American farmers began to look for a plant that was adaptable to prairie weather, and that could be trimmed into a hedge that was "pig-tight, horse-high, and bull-strong."
3. The tree, so named because it bore a large (but inedible) fruit the size of an orange, was among the sturdiest and hardiest of American trees, and was prized among Native Americans for the strength and flexibility of bows which were made from its wood.
4. The first people to practice agriculture on the American flatlands were faced with an important problem: what would they use to fence their land in a place that was almost entirely without trees or rocks?
5. Finally, an Illinois farmer brought the settlers a tree that was native to the land between the Red and Arkansas rivers, a tree called the Osage orange.

The best order is

A. 2 1 5 3 4
B. 1 2 3 4 5
C. 4 2 5 3 1
D. 4 2 1 3 5

Question 12   12._

1. After about ten minutes of such spirited and complicated activity, the head dancer is free to make up his or her own movements while maintaining the interest of the New Year's crowd.
2. The dancer will then perform a series of leg kicks, while at the same time operating the lion's mouth with his own hand and moving the ears and eyes by means of a string which is attached to the dancer's own mouth.
3. The most difficult role of this dance belongs to the one who controls the lion's head; this person must lead all the other "parts" of the lion through the choreographed segments of the dance.
4. The head dancer begins with a complex series of steps, alternately stepping forward with the head raised, and then retreating a few steps while lowering the head, a movement that is intended to create the impression that the lion is keeping a watchful eye for anything evil.
5. When performing a traditional Chinese New Year's lion dance, several performers must fit themselves inside a large lion costume and work together to enact different parts of the dance.

The best order is

A. 5 3 4 2 1
B. 3 4 2 5 1
C. 3 1 5 4 2
D. 4 2 3 5 1

Question 13

1. For many years the shell of the chambered nautilus was treasured in Europe for its beauty and intricacy, but collectors were unaware that they were in possession of the structure that marked a "missing link" in the evolution of marine mollusks.
2. The nautilus, however, evolved a series of enclosed chambers in its shell, and invented a new use for the structure: the shell began to serve as a buoyancy device.
3. Equipped with this new flotation device, the nautilus did not need the single, muscular foot of its predecessors, but instead developed flaps, tentacles, and a gentle form of jet propulsion that transformed it into the first mollusk able to take command of its own destiny and explore a three-dimensional world.
4. By pumping and adjusting air pressure into the chambers, the nautilus could spend the day resting on the bottom, and then rise toward the surface at night in search of food.
5. The nautilus shell looks like a large snail shell, similar to those of its ancestors, who used their shells as protective coverings while they were anchored to the sea floor.

The best order is

    A. 5 2 4 1 3
    B. 5 1 2 3 4
    C. 1 2 5 3 4
    D. 1 5 2 4 3

Question 14

1. While France and England battled for control of the region, the Acadiens prospered on the fertile farmland, which was finally secured by England in 1713.
2. Early in the 17th century, settlers from western France founded a colony called Acadie in what is now the Canadian province of Nova Scotia.
3. At this time, English officials feared the presence of spies among the Acadiens who might be loyal to their French homeland, and the Acadiens were deported to spots along the Atlantic and Caribbean shores of America.
4. The French settlers remained on this land, under English rule, for around forty years, until the beginning of the French and Indian War, another conflict between France and England.
5. As the Acadien refugees drifted toward a final home in southern Louisiana, neighbors shortened their name to "Cadien," and finally "Cajun," the name which the descendants of early Acadiens still call themselves.

The best order is

    A. 1 4 2 3 5
    B. 2 1 3 5 4
    C. 2 1 4 3 5
    D. 5 2 3 4 1

Question 15

15.__

1. Traditional households in the Eastern and Western regions of Africa serve two meals a day-one at around noon, and the other in the evening.
2. The starch is then used in the way that Americans might use a spoon, to scoop up a portion of the main dish on the person's plate.
3. The reason for the starch's inclusion in every meal has to do with taste as well as nutrition; African food can be very spicy, and the starch is known to cool the burning effect of the main dish.
4. When serving these meals, the main dish is usually served on individual plates, and the starch is served on a communal plate, from which diners break off a piece of bread or scoop rice or fufu in their fingers.
5. The typical meals usually consist of a thick stew or soup as the main course, and an accompanying starch–either bread, rice, *or fufu, a* starchy grain paste similar in consistency to mashed potatoes.

The best order is

    A. 5 2 3 4 1
    B. 5 1 4 3 2
    C. 1 4 5 3 2
    D. 1 5 4 2 3

Question 16

16.____

1. In the early days of the American Midwest, Indiana settlers sometimes came together to hold an event called an apple peeling, where neighboring settlers gathered at the homestead of a host family to help prepare the hosts' apple crop for cooking, canning, and making apple butter.
2. At the beginning of the event, each peeler sat down in front of a ten- or twenty-gallon stone jar and was given a crock of apples and a paring knife.
3. Once a peeler had finished with a crock, another was placed next to him; if the peeler was an unmarried man, he kept a strict count of the number of apples he had peeled, because the winner was allowed to kiss the girl of his choice.
4. The peeling usually ended by 9:30 in the evening, when the neighbors gathered in the host family's parlor for a dance social.
5. The apples were peeled, cored, and quartered, and then placed into the jar.

The best order is

    A. 1 5 3 4 2
    B. 2 5 3 4 1
    C. 1 2 5 3 4
    D. 2 1 5 4 3

Question 17

1. If your pet turtle is a land turtle and is native to temperate climates, it will stop eating some time in October, which should be your cue to prepare the turtle for hibernation.
2. The box should then be covered with a wire screen, which will protect the turtle from any rodents or predators that might want to take advantage of a motionless and helpless animal.
3. When your turtle hasn't eaten for a while and appears ready to hibernate, it should be moved to its winter quarters, most likely a cellar or garage, where the temperature should range between 40° and 45° F.
4. Instead of feeding the turtle, you should bathe it every day in warm water, to encourage the turtle to empty its intestines in preparation for its long winter sleep.
5. Here the turtle should be placed in a well-ventilated box whose bottom is covered with a moisture-absorbing layer of clay beads, and then filled three-fourths full with almost dry peat moss or wood chips, into which the turtle will burrow and sleep for several months.

The best order is

  A. 1 4 3 5 2
  B. 3 4 2 5 1
  C. 3 2 4 1 5
  D. 4 5 2 3 1

Question 18

1. Once he has reached the nest, the hunter uses two sturdy bamboo poles like huge chopsticks to pull the nest away from the mountainside, into a large basket that will be lowered to people waiting below.
2. The world's largest honeybees colonize the Nepalese mountainsides, building honeycombs as large as a person on sheer rock faces that are often hundreds of feet high.
3. In the remote mountain country of Nepal, a small band of "honey hunters" carry out a tradition so ancient that 10,000 year-old drawings of the practice have been found in the caves of Nepal.
4. To harvest the honey and beeswax from these combs, a honey hunter climbs above the nests, lowers a long bamboo-fiber ladder over the cliff, and then climbs down.
5. Throughout this dangerous practice, the hunter is stung repeatedly, and only the veterans, with skin that has been toughened over the years, are able to return from a hunt without the painful swelling caused by stings.

The best order is

  A. 2 4 3 5 1
  B. 2 4 1 5 3
  C. 5 3 2 4 1
  D. 3 2 4 1 5

Question 19   19.__

   1.   After the Romans left Britain, there were relentless attacks on the islands from the barbar-ian tribes of northern Germany—the Angles, Saxons, and Jutes.

   2.   As the empire weakened, Roman soldiers withdrew from Britain, leaving behind a country that continued to practice the Christian religion that had been introduced by the Romans.

   3.   Early Latin writings tell of a Christian warrior named Arturius (Arthur, in English) who led the British citizens to defeat these barbarian invaders, and brought an extended period of peace to the lands of Britain.

   4.   Long ago, the British Isles were part of the far-flung Roman Empire that extended across most of Europe and into Africa and Asia.

   5.   The romantic legend of King Arthur and his knights of the Round Table, one of the most popular and widespread stories of all time, appears to have some foundation in history.

The best order is

   A. 5 4 3 2 1
   B. 5 4 2 1 3
   C. 4 5 2 3 1
   D. 4 3 2 1 5

Question 20   20.__

   1.   The cylinder was allowed to cool until it sould stand on its own, and then it was cut from the tube and split down the side with a single straight cut.

   2.   Nineteenth-century glassmakers, who had not yet discovered the glazier's modern tech-niques for making panes of glass, had to create a method for converting their blown glass into flat sheets.

   3.   The bubble was then pierced at the end to make a hole that opened up while the glass-maker gently spun it, creating a cylinder of glass.

   4.   Turned on its side and laid on a conveyor belt, the cylinder was strengthened, or tempered, by being heated again and cooled very slowly, eventually flattening out into a single rectan-gular piece of glass.

   5.   To do this, the glassmaker dipped the end of a long tube into melted glass and blew into the other end of the tube, creating an expanding bubble of glass.

The best order is

   A. 2 5 3 4 1
   B. 2 4 5 3 1
   C. 3 5 2 4 1
   D. 3 1 4 5 2

Question 21

1. The splints are almost always hidden, but horses are occasionally born whose splinted toes project from the leg on either side, just above the hoof.
2. The second and fourth toes remained, but shrank to thin splints of bone that fused invisibly to the horse's leg bone.
3. Horses are unique among mammals, having evolved feet that each end in what is essentially a single toe, capped by a large, sturdy hoof.
4. Julius Caesar, an emperor of ancient Rome, was said to have owned one of these three-toed horses, and considered it so special that he would not permit anyone else to ride it.
5. Though the horse's earlier ancestors possessed the traditional mammalian set of five toes on each foot, the horse has retained only its third toe; its first and fifth toes disappeared completely as the horse evolved.

The best order is

A. 3 5 2 1 4
B. 5 3 2 4 1
C. 3 2 5 1 4
D. 5 2 3 1 4

Question 22

1. The new building materials—some of which are twenty feet long, and weigh nearly six tons—were transported to Pohnpei on rafts, and were brought into their present position by using hibiscus fiber ropes and leverage to move the stone columns upward along the inclined trunks of coconut palm trees.
2. The ancestors built great fires to heat the stone, and then poured cool seawater on the columns, which caused the stone to contract and split along natural fracture lines.
3. The now-abandoned enclave of Nan Madol, a group of 92 man-made islands off the shore of the Micronesian island of Pohnpei, is estimated to have been built around the year 500 A.D.
4. The islanders say their ancestors quarried stone columns from a nearby island, where large basalt columns were formed by the cooling of molten lava.
5. The structures of Nan Madol are remarkable for the sheer size of some of the stone "logs" or columns that were used to create the walls of the offshore community, and today anthropologists can only rely on the information of existing local people for clues about how Nan Madol was built.

The best order is

A. 5 4 3 2 1
B. 5 3 1 4 2
C. 3 5 4 2 1
D. 3 1 4 2 5

Question 23   23.__

   1.   One of the most easily manipulated substances on earth, glass can be made into ceramic tiles that are composed of over 90% air.

   2.   NASA's space shuttles are the first spacecraft ever designed to leave and re-enter the earth's atmosphere while remaining intact.

   3.   These ceramic tiles are such effective insulators that when a tile emerges from the oven in which it was fired, it can be held safely in a person's hand by the edges while its interior still glows at a temperature well over 2000° F.

   4.   Eventually, the engineers were led to a material that is as old as our most ancient civiliza-tionsglass.

   5.   Because the temperature during atmospheric re-entry is so incredibly hot, it took NASA's engineers some time to find a substance capable of protecting the shuttles.

The best order is

   A. 5 2 1 3 4
   B. 2 5 4 1 3
   C. 2 3 1 2 5
   D. 5 4 3 1 2

Question 24   24.__

   1.   The secret to teaching any parakeet to talk is patience, and the understanding that when a bird "talks," it is simply imitating what it hears, rather than putting ideas into words.

   2.   You should stay just out of sight of the bird and repeat the phrase you want it to learn, for at least fifteen minutes every morning and evening.

   3.   It is important to leave the bird without any words of encouragement or farewell; otherwise it might combine stray remarks or phrases, such as "Good night," with the phrase you are trying to teach it.

   4.   For this reason, to train your bird to imitate your words you should keep it free of any dis-tractions, especially other noises, while you are giving it "lessons."

   5.   After your repetition, you should quietly leave the bird alone for a while, to think over what it has just heard.

The best order is

   A. 1 4 2 5 3
   B. 1 2 4 3 5
   C. 3 2 1 5 4
   D. 3 1 5 4 2

Question 25

25.____

1. As a school approaches, fishermen from neighboring communities join their fishing boats together as a fleet, and string their gill nets together to make a huge fence that is held up by cork floats.

2. At a signal from the party leaders, or *nakura,* the family members pound the sides of the boats or beat the water with long poles, creating a sudden and deafening noise.

3. The fishermen work together to drag the trap into a half-circle that may reach 300 yards in diameter, and then the families move their boats to form the other half of the circle around the school of fish.

4. The school of fish flee from the commotion into the awaiting trap, where a final wall of net is thrown over the open end of the half-circle, securing the day's haul.

5. Indonesian people from the area around the Sulu islands live on the sea, in floating villages made of lashed-together or stilted homes, and make much of their living by fishing their home waters for migrating schools of snapper, scad, and other fish.

The best order is

A. 1 5 3 4 2
B. 1 2 4 3 5
C. 5 1 2 3 4
D. 5 1 3 2 4

———

KEY (CORRECT ANSWERS)

1.	D		11.	C
2.	D		12.	A
3.	B		13.	D
4.	A		14.	C
5.	C		15.	D
6.	C		16.	C
7.	D		17.	A
8.	D		18.	D
9.	A		19.	B
10.	B		20.	A

21.	A
22.	C
23.	B
24.	A
25.	D

———

PHILOSOPHY, PRINCIPLES, PRACTICES AND TECHNICS
OF
SUPERVISION, ADMINISTRATION, MANAGEMENT AND ORGANIZATION

TABLE OF CONTENTS

TABLE OF CONTENTS (CONTINUED)

PHILOSOPHY, PRINCIPLES, PRACTICES, AND TECHNICS
OF
SUPERVISION, ADMINISTRATION, MANAGEMENT AND ORGANIZATION

I. MEANING OF SUPERVISION

The extension of the democratic philosophy has been accompanied by an extension in the scope of supervision. Modern leaders and supervisors no longer think of supervision in the narrow sense of being confined chiefly to visiting employees, supplying materials, or rating the staff. They regard supervision as being intimately related to all the concerned agencies of society, they speak of the supervisor's function in terms of "growth", rather than the "improvement," of employees.

This modern concept of supervision may be defined as follows:

Supervision is leadership and the development of leadership within groups which are cooperatively engaged in inspection, research, training, guidance and evaluation.

II. THE OLD AND THE NEW SUPERVISION

TRADITIONAL
1. Inspection
2. Focused on the employee
3. Visitation
4. Random and haphazard
5. Imposed and authoritarian
6. One person usually

MODERN
1. Study and analysis
2. Focused on aims, materials, methods, supervisors, employees, environment
3. Demonstrations, intervisitation, workshops, directed reading, bulletins, etc.
4. Definitely organized and planned (scientific)
5. Cooperative and democratic
6. Many persons involved (creative)

III THE EIGHT (8) BASIC PRINCIPLES OF THE NEW SUPERVISION

1. *PRINCIPLE OF RESPONSIBILITY*
Authority to act and responsibility for acting must be joined.
   a. If you give responsibility, give authority.
   b. Define employee duties clearly.
   c. Protect employees from criticism by others.
   d. Recognize the rights as well as obligations of employees.
   e. Achieve the aims of a democratic society insofar as it is possible within the area of your work.
   f. Establish a situation favorable to training and learning.
   g. Accept ultimate responsibility for everything done in your section, unit, office, division, department.
   h. Good administration and good supervision are inseparable.

2. PRINCIPLE OF AUTHORITY
The success of the supervisor is measured by the extent to which the power of authority is no[t] used.
  a. Exercise simplicity and informality in supervision.
  b. Use the simplest machinery of supervision.
  c. If it is good for the organization as a whole, it is probably justified.
  d. Seldom be arbitrary or authoritative.
  e. Do not base your work on the power of position or of personality.
  f. Permit and encourage the free expression of opinions.

3. PRINCIPLE OF SELF-GROWTH
The success of the supervisor is measured by the extent to which, and the speed with which, he is no longer needed.
  a. Base criticism on principles, not on specifics.
  b. Point out higher activities to employees.
  c. Train for self-thinking by employees, to meet new situations.
  d. Stimulate initiative, self-reliance and individual responsibility.
  e. Concentrate on stimulating the growth of employees rather than on removing defects.

4. PRINCIPLE OF INDIVIDUAL WORTH
Respect for the individual is a paramount consideration in supervision.
  a. Be human and sympathetic in dealing with employees.
  b. Don't nag about things to be done.
  c. Recognize the individual differences among employees and seek opportunities to permit best expression of each personality.

5. PRINCIPLE OF CREATIVE LEADERSHIP
The best supervision is that which is not apparent to the employee.
  a. Stimulate, don't drive employees to creative action.
  b. Emphasize doing good things.
  c. Encourage employees to do what they do best.
  d. Do not be too greatly concerned with details of subject or method.
  e. Do not be concerned exclusively with immediate problems and activities.
  f. Reveal higher activities and make them both desired and maximally possible.
  g. Determine procedures in the light of each situation but see that these are derived from a sound basic philosophy.
  h. Aid, inspire and lead so as to liberate the creative spirit latent in all good employees.

6. PRINCIPLE OF SUCCESS AND FAILURE
There are no unsuccessful employees, only unsuccessful supervisors who have failed to give proper leadership.
  a. Adapt suggestions to the capacities, attitudes, and prejudices of employees.
  b. Be gradual, be progressive, be persistent.
  c. Help the employee find the general principle; have the employee apply his own problem to the general principle.
  d. Give adequate appreciation for good work and honest effort.
  e. Anticipate employee difficulties and help to prevent them.
  f. Encourage employees to do the desirable things they will do anyway.
  g. Judge your supervision by the results it secures.

7. PRINCIPLE OF SCIENCE

Successful supervision is scientific, objective, and experimental. It is based on facts, not on prejudices.

a. Be cumulative in results.
b. Never divorce your suggestions from the goals of training.
c. Don't be impatient of results.
d. Keep all matters on a professional, not a personal level.
e. Do not be concerned exclusively with immediate problems and activities.
f. Use objective means of determining achievement and rating where possible.

8. PRINCIPLE OF COOPERATION

Supervision is a cooperative enterprise between supervisor and employee.

a. Begin with conditions as they are.
b. Ask opinions of all involved when formulating policies.
c. Organization is as good as its weakest link.
d. Let employees help to determine policies and department programs.
e. Be approachable and accessible - physically and mentally.
f. Develop pleasant social relationships.

IV. WHAT IS ADMINISTRATION?

Administration is concerned with providing the environment, the material facilities, and the operational procedures that will promote the maximum growth and development of supervisors and employees. (Organization is an aspect, and a concomitant, of administration.)

There is no sharp line of demarcation between supervision and administration; these functions are intimately interrelated and, often, overlapping. They are complementary activities.

1. PRACTICES COMMONLY CLASSED AS "SUPERVISORY"

a. Conducting employees conferences
b. Visiting sections, units, offices, divisions, departments
c. Arranging for demonstrations
d. Examining plans
e. Suggesting professional reading
f. Interpreting bulletins
g. Recommending in-service training courses
h. Encouraging experimentation
i. Appraising employee morale
j. Providing for intervisitation

2. PRACTICES COMMONLY CLASSIFIED AS "ADMINISTRATIVE"

a. Management of the office
b. Arrangement of schedules for extra duties
c. Assignment of rooms or areas
d. Distribution of supplies
e. Keeping records and reports
f. Care of audio-visual materials
g. Keeping inventory records
h. Checking record cards and books
i. Programming special activities
j. Checking on the attendance and punctuality of employees

3. *PRACTICES COMMONLY CLASSIFIED AS BOTH "SUPERVISORY" AND "ADMINISTRATIVE"*
    a. Program construction
    b. Testing or evaluating outcomes
    c. Personnel accounting
    d. Ordering instructional materials

V. RESPONSIBILITIES OF THE SUPERVISOR

A person employed in a supervisory capacity must constantly be able to improve his own efficiency and ability. He represents the employer to the employees and only continuous self-examination can make him a capable supervisor.

Leadership and training are the supervisor's responsibility. An efficient working unit is one in which the employees work with the supervisor. It is his job to bring out the best in his employees. He must always be relaxed, courteous and calm in his association with his employees. Their feelings are important, and a harsh attitude does not develop the most efficient employees.

VI. COMPETENCIES OF THE SUPERVISOR

1. Complete knowledge of the duties and responsibilities of his position.
2. To be able to organize a job, plan ahead and carry through.
3. To have self-confidence and initiative.
4. To be able to handle the unexpected situation and make quick decisions.
5. To be able to properly train subordinates in the positions they are best suited for.
6. To be able to keep good human relations among his subordinates.
7. To be able to keep good human relations between his subordinates and himself and to earn their respect and trust.

VII. THE PROFESSIONAL SUPERVISOR-EMPLOYEE RELATIONSHIP

There are two kinds of efficiency: one kind is only apparent and is produced in organizations through the exercise of mere discipline; this is but a simulation of the second, or true, efficiency which springs from spontaneous cooperation. If you are a manager, no matter how great or small your responsibility, it is your job, in the final analysis, to create and develop this involuntary cooperation among the people whom you supervise. For, no matter how powerful a combination of money, machines, and materials a company may have, this is a dead and sterile thing without a team of willing, thinking and articulate people to guide it.

The following 21 points are presented as indicative of the exemplary basic relationship that should exist between supervisor and employee:

1. Each person wants to be liked and respected by his fellow employee and wants to be treated with consideration and respect by his superior.
2. The most competent employee will make an error. However, in a unit where good relations exist between the supervisor and his employees, tenseness and fear do not exist. Thus, errors are not hidden or covered up and the efficiency of a unit is not impaired.
3. Subordinates resent rules, regulations, or orders that are unreasonable or unexplained.
4. Subordinates are quick to resent unfairness, harshness, injustices and favoritism.
5. An employee will accept responsibility if he knows that he will be complimented for a job well done, and not too harshly chastised for failure; that his supervisor will check the cause of the failure, and, if it was the supervisor's fault, he will assume the blame therefore. If it was the employee's fault, his supervisor will explain the correct method or means of handling the responsibility.

6. An employee wants to receive credit for a suggestion he has made, that is used. If a suggestion cannot be used, the employee is entitled to an explanation. The supervisor should not say "no" and close the subject.
7. Fear and worry slow up a worker's ability. Poor working environment can impair his physical and mental health. A good supervisor avoids forceful methods, threats and arguments to get a job done.
8. A forceful supervisor is able to train his employees individually and as a team, and is able to motivate them in the proper channels.
9. A mature supervisor is able to properly evaluate his subordinates and to keep them happy and satisfied.
10. A sensitive supervisor will never patronize his subordinates.
11. A worthy supervisor will respect his employees' confidences.
12. Definite and clear-cut responsibilities should be assigned to each executive.
13. Responsibility should always be coupled with corresponding authority.
14. No change should be made in the scope or responsibilities of a position without a definite understanding to that effect on the part of all persons concerned.
15. No executive or employee, occupying a single position in the organization, should be subject to definite orders from more than one source.
16. Orders should never be given to subordinates over the head of a responsible executive. Rather than do this, the officer in question should be supplanted.
17. Criticisms of subordinates should, whoever possible, be made privately, and in no case should a subordinate be criticized in the presence of executives or employees of equal or lower rank.
18. No dispute or difference between executives or employees as to authority or responsibilities should be considered too trivial for prompt and careful adjudication.
19. Promotions, wage changes, and disciplinary action should always be approved by the executive immediately superior to the one directly responsible.
20. No executive or employee should ever be required, or expected, to be at the same time an assistant to, and critic of, another.
21. Any executive whose work is subject to regular inspection should, whever practicable, be given the assistance and facilities necessary to enable him to maintain an independent check of the quality of his work.

VIII. MINI-TEXT IN SUPERVISION, ADMINISTRATION, MANAGEMENT, AND ORGANIZATION

A. BRIEF HIGHLIGHTS

Listed concisely and sequentially are major headings and important data in the field for quick recall and review.

1. *LEVELS OF MANAGEMENT*

Any organization of some size has several levels of management. In terms of a ladder the levels are:

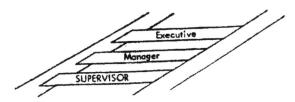

The first level is very important because it is the beginning point of management leadership.

2. WHAT THE SUPERVISOR MUST LEARN
A supervisor must learn to:
(1) Deal with people and their differences
(2) Get the job done through people
(3) Recognize the problems when they exist
(4) Overcome obstacles to good performance
(5) Evaluate the performance of people
(6) Check his own performance in terms of accomplishment

3. A DEFINITION OF SUPERVISOR
The term supervisor means any individual having authority, in the interests of the employer, to hire, transfer, suspend, lay-off, recall, promote, discharge, assign, reward, or discipline other employees or responsibility to direct them, or to adjust their grievances, or effectively to recommend such action, if, in connection with the foregoing, exercise of such authority is not of a merely routine or clerical nature but requires the use of independent judgment.

4. ELEMENTS OF THE TEAM CONCEPT
What is involved in teamwork? The component parts are:

(1) Members	(3) Goals	(5) Cooperation
(2) A leader	(4) Plans	(6) Spirit

5. PRINCIPLES OF ORGANIZATION
(1) A team member must know what his job is.
(2) Be sure that the nature and scope of a job are understood.
(3) Authority and responsibility should be carefully spelled out.
(4) A supervisor should be permitted to make the maximum number of decisions affecting his employees.
(5) Employees should report to only one supervisor.
(6) A supervisor should direct only as many employees as he can handle effectively.
(7) An organization plan should be flexible.
(8) Inspection and performance of work should be separate.
(9) Organizational problems should receive immediate attention.
(10) Assign work in line with ability and experience.

6. THE FOUR IMPORTANT PARTS OF EVERY JOB
(1) Inherent in every job is the *accountability* for results.
(2) A second set of factors in every job is *responsibilities.*
(3) Along with duties and responsibilities one must have the *authority* to act within certain limits without obtaining permission to proceed.
(4) No job exists in a vacuum. The supervisor is surrounded by key *relationships.*

7. PRINCIPLES OF DELEGATION
Where work is delegated for the first time, the supervisor should think in terms of these questions:
(1) Who is best qualified to do this?
(2) Can an employee improve his abilities by doing this?
(3) How long should an employee spend on this?
(4) Are there any special problems for which he will need guidance?
(5) How broad a delegation can I make?

8. PRINCIPLES OF EFFECTIVE COMMUNICATIONS

(1) Determine the media
(2) To whom directed?
(3) Identification and source authority
(4) Is communication understood?

9. PRINCIPLES OF WORK IMPROVEMENT

(1) Most people usually do only the work which is assigned to them
(2) Workers are likely to fit assigned work into the time available to perform it
(3) A good workload usually stimulates output
(4) People usually do their best work when they know that results will be reviewed or inspected
(5) Employees usually feel that someone else is responsible for conditions of work, workplace layout, job methods, type of tools/equipment, and other such factors
(6) Employees are usually defensive about their job security
(7) Employees have natural resistance to change
(8) Employees can support or destroy a supervisor
(9) A supervisor usually earns the respect of his people through his personal example of diligence and efficiency

10. AREAS OF JOB IMPROVEMENT

The areas of job improvement are quite numerous, but the most common ones which a supervisor can identify and utilize are:

(1) Departmental layout
(2) Flow of work
(3) Workplace layout
(4) Utilization of manpower
(5) Work methods
(6) Materials handling
(7) Utilization
(8) Motion economy

11. SEVEN KEY POINTS IN MAKING IMPROVEMENTS

(1) Select the job to be improved
(2) Study how it is being done now
(3) Question the present method
(4) Determine actions to be taken
(5) Chart proposed method
(6) Get approval and apply
(7) Solicit worker participation

12. CORRECTIVE TECHNIQUES OF JOB IMPROVEMENT

Specific Problems	General Improvement	Corrective Techniques
(1) Size of workload	(1) Departmental layout	(1) Study with scale model
(2) Inability to meet schedules	(2) Flow of work	(2) Flow chart study
(3) Strain and fatigue	(3) Work plan layout	(3) Motion analysis
(4) Improper use of men and skills	(4) Utilization of manpower	(4) Comparison of units produced to standard allowance
(5) Waste, poor quality, unsafe conditions	(5) Work methods	(5) Methods analysis
(6) Bottleneck conditions that hinder output	(6) Materials handling	(6) Flow chart & equipment study
(7) Poor utilization of equipment and machine	(7) Utilization of equipment	(7) Down time vs. running time
(8) Efficiency and productivity of labor	(8) Motion economy	(8) Motion analysis

13. A *PLANNING CHECKLIST*

(1) Objectives	(6) Resources	(11) Safety
(2) Controls	(7) Manpower	(12) Money
(3) Delegations	(8) Equipment	(13) Work
(4) Communications	(9) Supplies and materials	(14) Timing of improvements
(5) Resources	(10) Utilization of time	

14. *FIVE CHARACTERISTICS OF GOOD DIRECTIONS*

In order to get results, directions must be:

(1) Possible of accomplishment	(3) Related to mission	(5) Unmistakably clea
(2) Agreeable with worker interests	(4) Planned and complete	

15. *TYPES OF DIRECTIONS*

(1) Demands or direct orders	(3) Suggestion or implication
(2) Requests	(4) Volunteering

16. *CONTROLS*

A typical listing of the overall areas in which the supervisor should establish controls might be:

(1) Manpower	(3) Quality of work	(5) Time	(7) Money
(2) Materials	(4) Quantity of work	(6) Space	(8) Methods

17. *ORIENTING THE NEW EMPLOYEE*

(1) Prepare for him	(3) Orientation for the job
(2) Welcome the new employee	(4) Follow-up

18. *CHECKLIST FOR ORIENTING NEW EMPLOYEES*   Yes   No

(1) Do your appreciate the feelings of new employees when they first report for work?   ___ ___

(2) Are you aware of the fact that the new employee must make a big adjustment to his job?   ___ ___

(3) Have you given him good reasons for liking the job and the organization?   ___ ___

(4) Have you prepared for his first day on the job?   ___ ___

(5) Did you welcome him cordially and make him feel needed?

(6) Did you establish rapport with him so that he feels free to talk and discuss matters with you?   ___ ___

(7) Did you explain his job to him and his relationship to you?   ___ ___

(8) Does he know that his work will be evaluated periodically on a basis that is fair and objective?   ___ ___

(9) Did you introduce him to his fellow workers in such a way that they are likely to accept him?   ___ ___

(10) Does he know what employee benefits he will receive?

(11) Does he understand the importance of being on the job and what to do if he must leave his duty station?   ___ ___

(12) Has he been impressed with the importance of accident prevention and safe practice?   ___ ___

(13) Does he generally know his way around the department?   ___ ___

(14) Is he under the guidance of a sponsor who will teach the right ways of doing things?   ___ ___

(15) Do you plan to follow-up so that he will continue to adjust successfully to his job?   ___ ___

19. PRINCIPLES OF LEARNING
(1) Motivation   (2) Demonstration or explanation   (3) Practice

20. CAUSES OF POOR PERFORMANCE
(1) Improper training for job
(2) Wrong tools
(3) Inadequate directions
(4) Lack of supervisory follow-up
(5) Poor communications
(6) Lack of standards of performance
(7) Wrong work habits
(8) Low morale
(9) Other

21. FOUR MAJOR STEPS IN ON-THE-JOB INSTRUCTION
(1) Prepare the worker
(2) Present the operation
(3) Tryout performance
(4) Follow-up

22. EMPLOYEES WANT FIVE THINGS
(1) Security (2) Opportunity (3) Recognition (4) Inclusion (5) Expression

23. SOME DON'TS IN REGARD TO PRAISE
(1) Don't praise a person for something he hasn't done
(2) Don't praise a person unless you can be sincere
(3) Don't be sparing in praise just because your superior withholds it from you
(4) Don't let too much time elapse between good performance and recognition of it

24. HOW TO GAIN YOUR WORKERS' CONFIDENCE
Methods of developing confidence include such things as:
(1) Knowing the interests, habits, hobbies of employees
(2) Admitting your own inadequacies
(3) Sharing and telling of confidence in others
(4) Supporting people when they are in trouble
(5) Delegating matters that can be well handled
(6) Being frank and straightforward about problems and working conditions
(7) Encouraging others to bring their problems to you
(8) Taking action on problems which impede worker progress

25. SOURCES OF EMPLOYEE PROBLEMS
On-the-job causes might be such things as:
(1) A feeling that favoritism is exercised in assignments
(2) Assignment of overtime
(3) An undue amount of supervision
(4) Changing methods or systems
(5) Stealing of ideas or trade secrets
(6) Lack of interest in job
(7) Threat of reduction in force
(8) Ignorance or lack of communications
(9) Poor equipment
(10) Lack of knowing how supervisor feels toward employee
(11) Shift assignments

Off-the-job problems might have to do with:
(1) Health   (2) Finances   (3) Housing   (4) Family

26. THE SUPERVISOR'S KEY TO DISCIPLINE

There are several key points about discipline which the supervisor should keep in mind:

(1) Job discipline is one of the disciplines of life and is directed by the supervisor.
(2) It is more important to correct an employee fault than to fix blame for it.
(3) Employee performance is affected by problems both on the job and off.
(4) Sudden or abrupt changes in behavior can be indications of important employee problems.
(5) Problems should be dealt with as soon as possible after they are identified.
(6) The attitude of the supervisor may have more to do with solving problems than the techniques of problem solving.
(7) Correction of employee behavior should be resorted to only after the supervisor is sure that training or counseling will not be helpful.
(8) Be sure to document your disciplinary actions.
(9) Make sure that you are disciplining on the basis of facts rather than personal feelings.
(10) Take each disciplinary step in order, being careful not to make snap judgments, or decisions based on impatience.

27. FIVE IMPORTANT PROCESSES OF MANAGEMENT

(1) Planning   (2) Organizing   (3) Scheduling
(4) Controlling   (5) Motivating

28. WHEN THE SUPERVISOR FAILS TO PLAN

(1) Supervisor creates impression of not knowing his job
(2) May lead to excessive overtime
(3) Job runs itself -- supervisor lacks control
(4) Deadlines and appointments missed
(5) Parts of the work go undone
(6) Work interrupted by emergencies
(7) Sets a bad example
(8) Uneven workload creates peaks and valleys
(9) Too much time on minor details at expense of more important tasks

29. FOURTEEN GENERAL PRINCIPLES OF MANAGEMENT

(1) Division of work
(2) Authority and responsibility
(3) Discipline
(4) Unity of command
(5) Unity of direction
(6) Subordination of individual interest to general interest
(7) Remuneration of personnel
(8) Centralization
(9) Scalar chain
(10) Order
(11) Equity
(12) Stability of tenure of personnel
(13) Initiative
(14) Esprit de corps

30. CHANGE

Bringing about change is perhaps attempted more often, and yet less well understood, than anything else the supervisor does. How do people generally react to change? (People tend to resist change that is imposed upon them by other individuals or circumstances.

Change is characteristic of every situation. It is a part of every real endeavor where the efforts of people are concerned.

A. Why do people resist change?
    People may resist change because of:
        (1) Fear of the unknown
        (2) Implied criticism
        (3) Unpleasant experiences in the past
        (4) Fear of loss of status
        (5) Threat to the ego
        (6) Fear of loss of economic stability

B. How can we best overcome the resistance to change?
    In initiating change, take these steps:
        (1) Get ready to sell
        (2) Identify sources of help
        (3) Anticipate objections
        (4) Sell benefits
        (5) Listen in depth
        (6) Follow up

B. BRIEF TOPICAL SUMMARIES

I. WHO/WHAT IS THE SUPERVISOR?

1. The supervisor is often called the "highest level employee and the lowest level manager."
2. A supervisor is a member of both management and the work group. He acts as a bridge between the two.
3. Most problems in supervision are in the area of human relations, or people problems.
4. Employees expect: Respect, opportunity to learn and to advance, and a sense of belonging, and so forth.
5. Supervisors are responsible for directing people and organizing work. Planning is of paramount importance.
6. A position description is a set of duties and responsibilities inherent to a given position.
7. It is important to keep the position description up-to-date and to provide each employee with his own copy.

II. THE SOCIOLOGY OF WORK

1. People are alike in many ways; however, each individual is unique.
2. The supervisor is challenged in getting to know employee differences. Acquiring skills in evaluating individuals is an asset.
3. Maintaining meaningful working relationships in the organization is of great importance.
4. The supervisor has an obligation to help individuals to develop to their fullest potential.
5. Job rotation on a planned basis helps to build versatility and to maintain interest and enthusiasm in work groups.
6. Cross training (job rotation) provides backup skills.
7. The supervisor can help reduce tension by maintaining a sense of humor, providing guidance to employees, and by making reasonable and timely decisions. Employees respond favorably to working under reasonably predictable circumstances.
8. Change is characteristic of all managerial behavior. The supervisor must adjust to changes in procedures, new methods, technological changes, and to a number of new and sometimes challenging situations.
9. To overcome the natural tendency for people to resist change, the supervisor should become more skillful in initiating change.

III. PRINCIPLES AND PRACTICES OF SUPERVISION

1. Employees should be required to answer to only one superior.
2. A supervisor can effectively direct only a limited number of employees, depending upon the complexity, variety, and proximity of the jobs involved.
3. The organizational chart presents the organization in graphic form. It reflects lines of authority and responsibility as well as interrelationships of units within the organization.
4. Distribution of work can be improved through an analysis using the "Work Distribution Chart."
5. The "Work Distribution Chart" reflects the division of work within a unit in understandable form.
6. When related tasks are given to an employee, he has a better chance of increasing his skills through training.
7. The individual who is given the responsibility for tasks must also be given the appropriate authority to insure adequate results.
8. The supervisor should delegate repetitive, routine work. Preparation of recurring reports, maintaining leave and attendance records are some examples.
9. Good discipline is essential to good task performance. Discipline is reflected in the actions of employees on the job in the absence of supervision.
10. Disciplinary action may have to be taken when the positive aspects of discipline have failed. Reprimand, warning, and suspension are examples of disciplinary action.
11. If a situation calls for a reprimand, be sure it is deserved and remember it is to be done in private.

IV. DYNAMIC LEADERSHIP

1. A style is a personal method or manner of exerting influence.
2. Authoritarian leaders often see themselves as the source of power and authority.
3. The democratic leader often perceives the group as the source of authority and power.
4. Supervisors tend to do better when using the pattern of leadership that is most natural for them.
5. Social scientists suggest that the effective supervisor use the leadership style that best fits the problem or circumstances involved.
6. All four styles -- telling, selling, consulting, joining -- have their place. Using one does not preclude using the other at another time.
7. The theory X point of view assumes that the average person dislikes work, will avoid it whenever possible, and must be coerced to achieve organizational objectives.
8. The theory Y point of view assumes that the average person considers work to be as natural as play, and, when the individual is committed, he requires little supervision or direction to accomplish desired objectives.
9. The leader's basic assumptions concerning human behavior and human nature affect his actions, decisions, and other managerial practices.
10. Dissatisfaction among employees is often present, but difficult to isolate. The supervisor should seek to weaken dissatisfaction by keeping promises, being sincere and considerate, keeping employees informed, and so forth.
11. Constructive suggestions should be encouraged during the natural progress of the work.

V. PROCESSES FOR SOLVING PROBLEMS

1. People find their daily tasks more meaningful and satisfying when they can improve them.
2. The causes of problems, or the key factors, are often hidden in the background. Ability to solve problems often involves the ability to isolate them from their backgrounds. There is some substance to the cliché that some persons "can't see the forest for the trees."
3. New procedures are often developed from old ones. Problems should be broken down into manageable parts. New ideas can be adapted from old ones.

4. People think differently in problem-solving situations. Using a logical, patterned approach is often useful. One approach found to be useful includes these steps:

    (a) Define the problem   (d) Weigh and decide
    (b) Establish objectives   (e) Take action
    (c) Get the facts   (f) Evaluate action

VI. TRAINING FOR RESULTS

1. Participants respond best when they feel training is important to them.
2. The supervisor has responsibility for the training and development of those who report to him.
3. When training is delegated to others, great care must be exercised to insure the trainer has knowledge, aptitude, and interest for his work as a trainer.
4. Training (learning) of some type goes on continually. The most successful supervisor makes certain the learning contributes in a productive manner to operational goals.
5. New employees are particularly susceptible to training. Older employees facing new job situations require specific training, as well as having need for development and growth opportunities.
6. Training needs require continuous monitoring.
7. The training officer of an agency is a professional with a responsibility to assist supervisors in solving training problems.
8. Many of the self-development steps important to the supervisor's own growth are equally important to the development of peers and subordinates. Knowledge of these is important when the supervisor consults with others on development and growth opportunities.

VII. HEALTH, SAFETY, AND ACCIDENT PREVENTION

1. Management-minded supervisors take appropriate measures to assist employees in maintaining health and in assuring safe practices in the work environment.
2. Effective safety training and practices help to avoid injury and accidents.
3. Safety should be a management goal. All infractions of safety which are observed should be corrected without exception.
4. Employees' safety attitude, training and instruction, provision of safe tools and equipment, supervision, and leadership are considered highly important factors which contribute to safety and which can be influenced directly by supervisors.
5. When accidents do occur they should be investigated promptly for very important reasons, including the fact that information which is gained can be used to prevent accidents in the future.

VIII. EQUAL EMPLOYMENT OPPORTUNITY

1. The supervisor should endeavor to treat all employees fairly, without regard to religion, race, sex, or national origin.
2. Groups tend to reflect the attitude of the leader. Prejudice can be detected even in very subtle form. Supervisors must strive to create a feeling of mutual respect and confidence in every employee.
3. Complete utilization of all human resources is a national goal. Equitable consideration should be accorded women in the work force, minority-group members, the physically and mentally handicapped, and the older employee. The important question is: "Who can do the job?"
4. Training opportunities, recognition for performance, overtime assignments, promotional opportunities, and all other personnel actions are to be handled on an equitable basis.

IX. IMPROVING COMMUNICATIONS

1. Communications is achieving understanding between the sender and the receiver of a message. It also means sharing information -- the creation of understanding.
2. Communication is basic to all human activity. Words are means of conveying meanings; however, real meanings are in people.
3. There are very practical differences in the effectiveness of one-way, impersonal, and two-way communications. Words spoken face-to-face are better understood. Telephone conversations are effective, but lack the rapport of person-to-person exchanges. The whole person communicates.
4. Cooperation and communication in an organization go hand in hand. When there is a mutual respect between people, spelling out rules and procedures for communicating is unnecessary.
5. There are several barriers to effective communications. These include failure to listen with respect and understanding, lack of skill in feedback, and misinterpreting the meanings of words used by the speaker. It is also common practice to listen to what we want to hear, and tune out things we do not want to hear.
6. Communication is management's chief problem. The supervisor should accept the challenge to communicate more effectively and to improve interagency and intra-agency communications.
7. The supervisor may often plan for and conduct meetings. The planning phase is critical and may determine the success or the failure of a meeting.
8. Speaking before groups usually requires extra effort. Stage fright may never disappear completely, but it can be controlled.

X. SELF-DEVELOPMENT

1. Every employee is responsible for his own self-development.
2. Toastmaster and toastmistress clubs offer opportunities to improve skills in oral communications.
3. Planning for one's own self-development is of vital importance. Supervisors know their own strengths and limitations better than anyone else.
4. Many opportunities are open to aid the supervisor in his developmental efforts, including job assignments; training opportunities, both governmental and non-governmental -- to include universities and professional conferences and seminars.
5. Programmed instruction offers a means of studying at one's own rate.
6. Where difficulties may arise from a supervisor's being away from his work for training, he may participate in televised home study or correspondence courses to meet his self-develop- ment needs.

XI. TEACHING AND TRAINING

A. The Teaching Process

Teaching is encouraging and guiding the learning activities of students toward established goals. In most cases this process consists in five steps: preparation, presentation, summarization, evaluation, and application.

1. Preparation

Preparation is twofold in nature; that of the supervisor and the employee.

Preparation by the supervisor is absolutely essential to success. He must know what, when, where, how, and whom he will teach. Some of the factors that should be considered are:

(1) The objectives	(5) Employee interest
(2) The materials needed	(6) Training aids
(3) The methods to be used	(7) Evaluation
(4) Employee participation	(8) Summarization

Employee preparation consists in preparing the employee to receive the material. Probably the most important single factor in the preparation of the employee is arousing and maintaining his interest. He must know the objectives of the training, why he is there, how the material can be used, and its importance to him.

2. Presentation

In presentation, have a carefully designed plan and follow it.

The plan should be accurate and complete, yet flexible enough to meet situations as they arise. The method of presentation will be determined by the particular situation and objectives.

3. Summary

A summary should be made at the end of every training unit and program. In addition, there may be internal summaries depending on the nature of the material being taught. The important thing is that the trainee must always be able to understand how each part of the new material relates to the whole.

4. Application

The supervisor must arrange work so the employee will be given a chance to apply new knowledge or skills while the material is still clear in his mind and interest is high. The trainee does not really know whether he has learned the material until he has been given a chance to apply it. If the material is not applied, it loses most of its value.

5. Evaluation

The purpose of all training is to promote learning. To determine whether the training has been a success or failure, the supervisor must evaluate this learning.

In the broadest sense evaluation includes all the devices, methods, skills, and techniques used by the supervisor to keep him self and the employees informed as to their progress toward the objectives they are pursuing. The extent to which the employee has mastered the knowledge, skills, and abilities, or changed his attitudes, as determined by the program objectives, is the extent to which instruction has succeeded or failed.

Evaluation should not be confined to the end of the lesson, day, or program but should be used continuously. We shall note later the way this relates to the rest of the teaching process.

B. Teaching Methods

A teaching method is a pattern of identifiable student and instructor activity used in presenting training material.

All supervisors are faced with the problem of deciding which method should be used at a given time.

As with all methods, there are certain advantages and disadvantages to each method.

1. Lecture

The lecture is direct oral presentation of material by the supervisor. The present trend is to place less emphasis on the trainer's activity and more on that of the trainee.

2. Discussion

Teaching by discussion or conference involves using questions and other techniques to arouse interest and focus attention upon certain areas, and by doing so creating a learning situation. This can be one of the most valuable methods because it gives the employees 'an opportunity to express their ideas and pool their knowledge.

3. Demonstration

The demonstration is used to teach how something works or how to do something. It can be used to show a principle or what the results of a series of actions will be. A well-staged demonstration is particularly effective because it shows proper methods of performance in a realistic manner.

4. Performance

Performance is one of the most fundamental of all learning techniques or teaching methods. The trainee may be able to tell how a specific operation should be performed but he cannot be sure he knows how to perform the operation until he has done so.

5. Which Method to Use

Moreover, there are other methods and techniques of teaching. It is difficult to use any method without other methods entering into it. In any learning situation a combination of methods is usually more effective than anyone method alone.

Finally, evaluation must be integrated into the other aspects of the teaching-learning process.

It must be used in the motivation of the trainees; it must be used to assist in developing understanding during the training; and it must be related to employee application of the results of training.

This is distinctly the role of the supervisor.

———